VINTAGE RAILTOURS

VINTAGE RAILTOURS

Railway Correspondence and Travel Society

A pictorial record 1954-69

Gavin Morrison

Silver Link Publishing Ltd

© Gavin Morrison 1993

First published in May 1993

British Library Cataloguing in Publication Data

Morrison, G. W.
    Vintage Railtours: Railway Correspondence and
    Travel Society - A Pictorial Record, 1954-69
    I. Title
    385.0941

ISBN 1 85794 007 5

Silver Link Publishing Ltd
Unit 5
Home Farm Close
Church Street
Wadenhoe
Peterborough PE8 5TE
Tel/fax (08015) 4-4-0

Printed and bound in Great Britain

The West Riding branch Dalesman Tour of 4 May 1963 is seen here passing Poole in Wharfedale. Apart from the lack of signals in the picture, I have always liked it for all the details it shows of a typical rural non-main-line station. At this point the tour was still nearly on time, but problems were to come, as described later. The locomotive is Gresley 'K4' 2-6-0 No 3442 *The Great Marquess*, owned by Lord Garnock and based in Leeds. The station was opened in February 1856, and finally lost its services on 22 March 1965, nearly two years after the tour. The site is now an exclusive residential estate. The photograph was obtained by kind permission of a local resident who allowed me to stand in the middle of one of her rosebeds to get to the railings and look over the wall. *Gavin Morrison*

Contents

Two of the seven locomotives used on the West Riding branch Borders Rail Tour on 9 July 1961 were preserved North British No 256 *Glen Douglas* and North British 'J37' 0-6-0 No 64624 of St Margarets depot. These locomotives operated the tour over the branch lines in the Borders, one of which was the Roxburgh to Jedburgh line where the train is seen approaching the station. Full details of this memorable tour are given elsewhere in the book. *Gavin Morrison*

Foreword

by Rodney Lissenden, Chairman, RCTS

In September 1927 a small group of railway enthusiasts gathered in a garden shed in Cheltenham Spa. This group decided to form themselves into a club and the Cheltenham Spa Railway Society was duly founded. After a few months the members agreed that the title lacked national appeal, and in January 1928 the present name, 'The Railway Correspondence and Travel Society', was adopted.

The background to the title of the Society stemmed from an early scheme whereby there would be 'full' members and 'corresponding' members, probably deriving in some way from the model railway activities of the Cheltenham Railway Club. This scheme seems never to have come to anything, but never the less it left its mark in the title.

The 'Travel' part is also an echo from over 60 years ago when rail versus road competition was on everyone's mind. On the front of the journal every member of the new Society was enjoined in bold capitals to 'Travel by and Rely on the Rail'.

The Society from the beginning produced a news sheet, *The Rail News*; this title was changed to the *Railway Observer* after a year. It first appeared as a duplicated sheet and the first printed issue appeared in 1932. The *RO* has been produced monthly by a band of volunteer editors, overseen by a Chief Editor, since 1932 and during that time has the proud record of never missing an issue despite effects of such things as war and strikes. The magazine is circulated to all members as part of the annual subscription.

The Society grew rapidly in the early years and in 1931 the administration moved to London where much of the work was conducted from members' homes. As membership expanded a branch network throughout the UK was set up with the intention of giving members local meetings and visits of railway interest. In April 1943 a Middle East branch was formed by members on active service. Its meetings, held in Cairo, preserved the pre-war Friday evening club night traditions of the Society! The Society currently has over 4,000 members worldwide, with membership numbers approaching 20,000. Meetings are held in over 20 centres, offering lectures, slide and film shows.

In 1935 the Society produced its first publication, the *Locomotive Stock Book*, a comprehensive list of locomotives at work in Great Britain - this was the first publication of its type and created a consider-

able sensation in the railway world at the time. From this early beginning the Society has become well known for its publications on locomotive histories, and has the reputation for accurate and authentic railway literature. Locomotive histories of the GWR in a series of 13 books, the LNER in a series of 18 books, and 10 books covering all constituent companies of the SR have been produced over many years. Currently the histories of the locomotives of the LMS and BR Standard Classes are being produced. Probably the Society's most successful book ever produced has been Part 2A of *Locomotives of the LNER*, dealing with the 'Pacific' classes, of which nearly 15,000 copies have been sold.

Although the phrase 'railtour' had not been coined in Britain in 1938, there is no doubt that the concept of a specially chartered train, privately planned and organised by railway enthusiasts in conjunction with the railway authorities originated with the RCTS tour using the Stirling 'Single' on 11 September 1938. The LNER tickets issued for the occasion were a half-day excursion with the title 'The Old Flying Scotsman Correspondence and Travel Society'. The train consisted of the old Stirling 'Single' No 1 of the GNR with seven vintage six-wheeled coaches which had been refurbished by the LNER in connection with the introduction of a new 'Flying Scotsman' train in June of that year. The tour ran from King's Cross to Peterborough and back and was filled with Society members and friends.

The 1939-45 war prevented any further excursions until 25 May 1946, when the Longmoor Military Railway was visited. It was on 30 September 1950 that a tour on the newly nationalised British Railways system ran from Holborn Viaduct to Victoria using three different locomotives. The Society's 'trademark' locomotive, SR 'Schools' Class No 30925 *Cheltenham*, was used on many tours over the years, as were many other famous locomotives. A large number of tours were run with the last active locomotive of a class, specially prepared and cleaned for a farewell journey. Many were run to record the closing of lines and, in many cases, the Society ran the last train to traverse a line.

The most ambitious tours run by the Society were the two-day Aberdeen Flyer in 1962, the five-day North Eastern in 1963 and a ten-day tour of Ireland in 1964. The latter year was the peak of activity for the Society's railtour programme, when no fewer than 24 tours were run.

The end of steam could not pass unnoticed and the Society ran a Farewell to Steam tour on 4 August 1968. The Society has continued to run tours using DMU and EMU stock as well as diesel and electric locomotives. The use of the 'Brighton Belle' on a commemorative tour was so popular that it had to be run twice in March 1972.

The Society has run over 300 tours in 64 years of existence and it was a great pleasure when Gavin Morrison suggested that this book be compiled illustrating some of these tours. The Society has given great pleasure to thousands of tour participants over the years, and this book must pay tribute to those Society officers who spent many hours on routes, itineraries and letter writing, and to British Rail for their help and co-operation over the years.

A final 'thank you' to Gavin, a long-standing Society member, for putting this selection together.

A ticket for the RCTS's first railtour on 11 September 1938. *RCTS*

Introduction

If you are a reader of the current railway magazines, you could be forgiven for believing that railtours were a relatively new phenomenon, probably dating from the return of steam to British Rail in 1971. This couldn't be further from the truth.

Railtours go back as far as 1938, when the famous Great Northern Stirling 'Single' No 1 was taken out of retirement at the old York Railway Museum and restored to working order to work a demonstration train from King's Cross to Stevenage on 30 June, comparing the 'Flying Scotsman' of 1888 with that of 1938. It had a further outing in August to Cambridge, followed by the first Railway Correspondence and Travel Society special on 11 September to Peterborough. So railtours came into being.

Naturally the war cut short any expansion of this leisure activity, but the idea had been established, and by 1950 railtours started to appear again on a regular basis. The number of societies involved in railtours also grew, names like the Locomotive Club of Great Britain (LCGB), the Stephenson Locomotive Society (SLS), Home Counties railtours, and the Ian Allan organisation, to name but a few, and on several occasions the societies joined forces and promoted joint tours.

Whilst visiting the Redmire branch on 2 January 1993 to witness the very last train on the line, I reflected how almost 29 years earlier - in fact April 1964 - I had been present to photograph the last train on the same line, but on what was then the extension to Hawes from Redmire. I concluded that the reasons for running tours have not really changed over the years - line closures and last runs of classes are still as good reasons as ever, but what has altered is the involvement of preserved steam locomotives, and possibly in 1993 preserved diesels.

In the days of BR steam the demise of a class usually involved one or possibly two specials. Now the last of a diesel class seems to go on for ever - for example, the Class '50s' seem to have been running last tours for almost a year. Not that I am complaining. . .!

The railtour business environment has changed in some respects. There is a tendency today for railtours, for a variety of reasons, to be organised by what in effect are a few professionally run businesses. However, the enthusiast-organised tour still exists, usually run by those dedicated few who put so much

time, effort and money into using tours as a means of raising funds to support their preserved locomotives, or to raise cash to buy them in the future. To those people the enthusiasts of today and tomorrow owe a great deal.

The Railway Correspondence and Travel Society has gained an enviable reputation over the years for the excellent and very detailed books it has produced on locomotives and other railway subjects. My objective in producing this album is not to delve into history in detail, or to give explanations on locomotive design technicalities, but to try and portray to the reader by word and photograph the great fun that was had by all on these tours, and, by comparison with today, with all the rules and safety regulations in force, what a free and friendly atmosphere prevailed on them.

As mentioned elsewhere, I have been a member of the Society for 36 years, and it came as a great surprise to me, when I started to look into the RCTS railtours in detail, that the Society had organised no fewer than 300 specials over the years. It was not until the 59th tour, the Yorkshire Coast Tour of 23 June 1957, that I first sampled the delights of an RCTS tour, and what a splendid outing it was; it is featured in more detail elsewhere in the book.

Travelling on the tours with organised photographic stops can make photography difficult for obvious reasons, and whilst preparing this album I have come to wish that I had spent as much time and effort photographing the antics of the passengers trying to get *their* pictures as I did just photographing the train and the locomotives. As my fellow West Riding branch committee members will recall, I was nearly always the last back on the train, trying to get that exclusive photograph with nobody in the picture! To those of you who have video cameras and travel on the current tours, maybe the passengers taking their pictures from all sorts of unlikely angles and locations might produce something more interesting for the future than just the locomotive hauling the train.

I always had the problem of deciding whether to travel on the tour or follow it by car and get as many pictures as possible. In the very early 1960s my red Volkswagen Beetle car was followed with interest by many of the passengers on the tours, especially around the north of the country. How times have changed on the roads - railtours, especially steam ones, are now a guarantee of traffic jams. I vividly remember following the last steam special over the West Highland line from Glasgow Queen Street to Mallaig, with *Glen Douglas* and various 'J37s' as motive power. Besides myself there were only two other vehicles following the train, one a little green A35 van, and the late W. J. V. Anderson in his Sunbeam Rapier. It was a very memorable day, with three locomotive failures and the failure of my car, which expired at Tyndrum - but courtesy of the local signalman it was sorted out after I had explained that the engine was at the rear and not the front!

There were many memorable if somewhat hectic journeys involved in obtaining the pictures that feature in this album, including day trips to the Isle of Wight and Swanage from Yorkshire - and this was long before the days of motorways. These trips often covered around 650 miles in the day.

With hindsight, which we all know is a wonderful thing, I sometimes feel I spent too much time photographing the specials rather than covering the everyday railway operation, a lesson I still don't seem to have learned by the 1990s, but the important thing was that I thoroughly enjoyed it.

Railway enthusiasts always have a tendency to look at the past through rose-tinted glasses, with a belief that the past was always better than the present, but I am convinced that I was fortunate enough to be around during the golden years of steam railtours. The pattern of the tours did change over the years, from straightforward outings with local engines working the last trains on lines to the bringing of spectacular motive power from one end of the country to another to work over what was, so to speak, the opposition's main lines. An example of the latter was the Solway Ranger, when the RCTS's West Riding branch obtained 'Merchant Navy' No 35012 for the tour which started at Leeds and travelled over Shap and the Settle and Carlisle line, until gradually the end of steam approached and the choice of motive power diminished to a few classes.

One could not have believed during the days of steam that such a following would develop for diesels and electrics. This so-called 'modern traction', which is now in many cases anything but modern, often around 30 years old, has developed a great following, and I for one am delighted that it has happened. Many of the current classes running on British Rail have enjoyed twice as many years of service as the hundreds of steam locomotives built after nationalisation.

Fifty tours out of a total of 300 is only scratching the surface, but that number was selected as being the optimum to feature in a book of this size. I hope the few words on each tour will serve to remind the

thousands who travelled on the specials of the delights, and in some cases disappointments, and to convey to the enthusiasts who were not around at the time what an exciting period we enjoyed in the 1950s and 1960s. I don't feel I could single out one tour as the one I enjoyed the most, or for that matter the least, but the few words I have written will give some indications.

Whilst writing the notes on the tours, it has reminded me of certain incidents which for obvious reasons I would be wrong to record in detail - for example, the day the West Riding branch committee stopped a tour in the late evening in the middle of nowhere to remove an unauthorised person from the footplate, a person who is now a very senior member of British Rail. Then there was the terrible row that developed between the driver and fireman on one tour, which nearly resulted in the latter leaving the train at a stop, not to mention the awful trouble a driver got into for negotiating a 30 mph restriction at over 50 mph, and many other less dramatic instances.

None of this could have happened without the goodwill of all the people in British Rail who were involved in one way or another in organising these tours. The various RCTS branches that ran tours regularly got to know their local BR people very well, and in many cases became good friends. In my own branch in the West Riding they included people like the Shed Masters at Holbeck and other local depots, the local Locomotive Inspectors, those in the Operating Departments as well as the offices who always willingly gave that little bit extra help to make the tours a success - to all of them on behalf of myself and the Society, our genuine thanks.

Finally I would like to feel that this album could be accepted as a token of thanks from the thousands who travelled on the specials to all the Society members who put the time and effort into running the tours, who usually on the day were too involved to be able to relax and enjoy the journey.

To the Society's Chairman, Rodney Lissenden, I extend a special thanks for all his help in the early stages of the preparation of the book, and for writing the history of the Society in his Foreword, and who, with fellow Society stalwart Hugh Ballantyne, has made his excellent photographs readily available for publication.

I must also not forget to express my thanks to all those who wrote the reports on the tours for the Society's magazine, *the Railway Observer*, without which I would have been at a loss to cover the specials on which I did not travel or photograph.

Although the Society is not currently involved in the railtour scene, it is still extremely active with

The final day of operation of the spectacular Stainmore line was Saturday 20 January 1962. The North Eastern branch of the Society organised the farewell tour, which was arranged so that it was the last train to travel over the summit. The locomotives rostered for the special were Standard '3MT' No 77003 and '4MT' No 76049, both classes having been regular performers on the line. The special is shown passing the delightful country station of Ravenstonedale on the section between Kirkby Stephen and Tebay. *Gavin Morrison*

over 4,000 members, and branches holding regular meetings at various venues throughout the country, covering subjects that should cater for all interests. If you don't happen to be a member, you might like to consider joining.

Gavin Morrison

16 May 1954   Lincolnshire Tour

This was an East Midlands branch tour from Nottingham Midland to the Lincolnshire countryside. The 210 passengers filled the five-coach train, and Nottingham depot (16A) had given one of their 'Compounds', No 40935, a good polish. The locomotive performed well to Lincoln, with a maximum of 62 mph before the arrival at St Mark's station.

At Lincoln the 'Compound' was exchanged for Great Northern 'J6' 0-6-0 No 64199 with a Lincoln crew and Inspector. The tour then set off into the land of somersault signals to Bardney, where the locomotive visited the small shed to water and turn.

The next stage was to take the long way round to Willoughby via Mablethorpe and Sutton-on-Sea, then on to Firsby where the tour joined the branch

to Spilsby, which had lost its passenger service 15 years previously. The Station Master gave the tour a warm welcome with a specially prepared sign and a bouquet of flowers; the latter was presented to the wife of the branch secretary, Mrs Forster.

From Firsby - where passengers noticed a board proclaiming the 'Temperance Refreshment Room' - the 'J6' headed for Bellwater Junction, Woodhall Junction, and then up the branch to Horncastle. After this the tour returned to Lincoln where 'Compound' No 40935 was waiting to head the train back to Nottingham.

A fine run saw the special back in under 40 minutes, just a few minutes early, with a maximum speed of 63 mph.

The effort put in by Nottingham depot to clean 'Compound' No 40935 is well shown in this picture of the train waiting to leave Midland station. The lined black livery looked extremely smart on the class, as it did on most other locomotives.

No 40935 was one of the last five of the class to be built at Derby in 1932. The first 'Compound' to be withdrawn was No 41171 in 1952, whilst the last to survive was No 41168, until 1961. *Hugh Ballantyne*

Above 'J6' No 64199 is nicely framed by the bridge at Dinnington on Bain; the 38A (Colwick) shedplate is clearly visible. Colwick always had a large allocation of this class, which it is reported were always very popular with the crews for either working coal or passenger duties in the Nottingham and Lincolnshire areas. Built as No 3550 at Doncaster in November 1925, No 64199 was withdrawn from traffic in April 1958. *Hugh Ballantyne*

Left Another view of No 64199, this time at Spilsby. *Hugh Ballantyne*

6 February 1955   The Hampshireman

As the photographs show, it was a fine sunny day that greeted the 540 passengers who descended on Waterloo to join this tour.

A good variety of motive power was rostered, with 'Brighton' 'Atlantic' No 32421 *South Foreland*, driven by Society member Bert Hooker of Nine Elms, who many years later was to give us the epic journey over Shap and the Settle and Carlisle line with 'Merchant Navy' No 35012 (see page 119). The 'Atlantic' was followed by two 'E5X' 0-6-2Ts, Nos 32570 and 32576 of Horsham shed, and finally two of the famous 'T9s', Nos 30301 and 30132, back to Waterloo.

The tour was well timed, as it allowed the passengers to travel on the last train over some of the lines which had officially closed the previous day. These included the Pulborough-Midhurst, Midhurst-Petersfield and Fareham-Alton lines. Needless to say the tour attracted much local interest with many members of the public turning out to see the train pass, not to mention a BBC news person who recorded an interview with the Society Chairman, Mr C. Smith.

The route was as follows: Waterloo to Woking via Barnes, Feltham, Staines, Chertsey and West Weybridge, and then to Guildford; Guildford to Horsham (reverse) then via Christ's Hospital to Pulborough, Midhurst and Petersfield; onwards via Havant, Fareham, Fontley Tunnel and the Meon Valley line, Alton, Aldershot, and Frimley, where a reversal was made to Farnborough; and back via the main line to Waterloo with the 'T9s'.

The Class 'E5' tanks were built by the London, Brighton & South Coast Railway in 1903 and 1904, and were excellent locomotives if not worked too hard. In 1911 four members of the class were converted to 'E5X', the rebuilding altering the appearance considerably. The locomotives were originally named, Nos 32576 and 32570 having been *Brenchley* and *Armington* respectively. No 32570 was the last of the 'E5Xs' to survive, being withdrawn less than a year after the tour, in January 1956, with a claimed mileage of 1,332,546 in traffic. The two immaculate locomotives are shown here at Horsham. *Hugh Ballantyne*

Sporting an extremely prominent headboard, and with no fewer than three RCTS badges on the front, No 32576 pauses at Midhurst. Note the Inspector, complete with his bowler hat, leaning out of the cab. *Hugh Ballantyne*

Ready to leave Petersfield for Waterloo, the two 'T9s', Nos 30301 and 30732, await the 'right away'. The locomotives were not nicknamed 'Greyhounds' for nothing - there were many instances in the 1950s where they took over from bigger failed locomotives and put up superb performances. The last one to be overhauled was No 30707 as late as March 1959, which was surprising as many had already been withdrawn. In fact, the two tour locomotives lasted until August and October 1959 respectively. One member of the class, No 30717, is recorded as having covered more than 2 million miles, and several others were very close to this figure. By the winter of 1960-61 only No 30707 was working east of Exeter, being replaced in March by No 30117, but by July they were all withdrawn, except No 120 which happily survived into preservation, and is currently to be seen on the Swanage Railway. *Hugh Ballantyne*

24 July 1955 The Fensman

This six-coach tour started at London Liverpool Street and, as can be seen in the photograph, Stratford Depot turned out an immaculate 'Britannia', No 70037 *Hereward the Wake*. With a train weight of only 210 tons, the 'Pacific' was able to give the 200 passengers some lively running to Audley End, where it was replaced by well-groomed 'J17' 0-6-0 No 65562.

The impressive headboard was appropriately based on the heraldic device of the Great Ouse River Board, the successors of the Bedford Level Corporation, which was responsible for the greater part of the little-known fenland area which the tour visited.

The 'J17' set off from Audley End to Bartlow via Saffron Walden, then via the Cambridge goods line to Mildenhall. Returning thence to Fordham and on to Ely, the tour then turned northwards to Denver for a trip along the branch to Stoke Ferry. The train then made its way south again via Ely and westwards to St Ives, returning northwards once more to visit the branch to Ramsey before heading for Cambridge.

The 'J17s' were seldom used on passenger work but No 65562 gave a first-class performance with speeds in the mid-50s being attained several times on the tour. The fireman on the 0-6-0 was in fact a Society member who no doubt encouraged the driver and Inspector to see what the locomotive could do. The 'Britannia' then returned to Liverpool Street on a fast schedule.

The immaculate condition in which Stratford Depot (30A) kept the 'Britannias' in 1950 was in sharp contrast to the way most of the class finished their working days on the London Midland Region at Kingmoor depot.

No 70037 *Hereward the Wake* was the 'Pacific' chosen to head the Fensman tour from Liverpool Street. It entered traffic in December 1952 on the Great Eastern main line, but by November 1966 its working days were finished. Only a few weeks prior to the tour it had been used on the up 'Scandinavian', when King Frederick of Denmark was travelling in a Royal saloon. *Hugh Ballantyne*

Above It is possible that the Fensman tour might have been the main event in the working life of 'J17' No 65562. Built at Stratford as a Great Eastern Class 'G58' in April 1905, the locomotive survived until August 1958, and is seen here at Stoke Ferry. *Hugh Ballantyne*

Left Another picture of No 65562, this time at Ramsey East. *Hugh Ballantyne*

9 September 1956   Fensman No 2

This was an ambitious tour as it ran in two portions for part of the itinerary. From London King's Cross the six-coach portion was headed by immaculate 'K3' No 61942 from Stratford depot, whilst from Nottingham another well-turned out 'Mogul', 'Crab' No 42784, headed the second portion. The meeting point was Peterborough, where the two portions combined into a ten-coach train with 310 passengers on board.

At Peterborough 'B1' 4-6-0 No 61391 took over from the 'Moguls' and headed the special to Whittlesea. Here the passengers exchanged the comfort of the coaches for 15 vacuum-fitted open wagons plus two brake-vans for a trip on the Benwick branch. 'J17' No 65562, which had performed so well on the Fensman trip the previous year, was the motive power for what was believed to be the first ever fare-paying passenger train down this branch.

The 'B1' then continued the tour to Wisbech via March West curve, and once again the participants took to the open for a ride on the Wisbech & Upwell Tramway, headed by diesel No 11102.

The tour then continued to Sleaford North Junction where the 'B1' was exchanged for Gresley 'K2' 'Mogul' No 61743. From Spalding the branch to Bourne was taken, where the train reversed before heading back towards Spalding. Here the two portions of the train were separated, and headed back to Nottingham and London respectively with the original motive power.

Stratford depot had as always turned out tour locomotives in superb external condition. 'K3' No 61942 is seen prior to departure inside King's Cross, and represented a class seldom seen on passenger work at this location in the 1950s. When built in October 1935 the locomotive was numbered 2451, and was one of the batch built by the North British Loco Co. It survived until November 1962. *Hugh Ballantyne*

Left No 61942 is next seen in the yard alongside Peterborough North Box before handing over to 'B1' No 61391, which then took over the two combined portions of the tour. *Hugh Ballantyne*

Below The 15 open wagons and two brake-vans were virtually filled to capacity by the 310 passengers on the tour. 'J17' No 65562, not so well turned out as on the previous Fensman tour of 24 July 1955, is shown at Benwick. *Hugh Ballantyne*

Above The tour at Wisbech prior to departure for a ride on the Wisbech & Upwell Tramway. Drewry diesel No 11102 heads the train, one of a class of three built in May 1952 which were eventually numbered D2200-D2202. The trio survived until April 1968. *Hugh Ballantyne*

Right The tour enjoyed three different types of 'Moguls' as motive power, namely 'K3', 'Crab' and 'K2'. The 'K2', No 61743, is seen at the head of the special as it prepares to leave Sleaford. Note the signal which is positioned through the station roof.

The locomotive was built at Doncaster in June 1916 and was eventually withdrawn in June 1959. At the time of the tour it was allocated to Boston along with roughly a dozen other members of the class.

The locomotives are probably best remembered for their work on the West Highland line, which was in sharp contrast to the duties they performed for many years around the Nottingham and Lincoln areas. *Hugh Ballantyne*

Sunday 28 April 1957
North Somerset Rail Tour

In spite of the fact that this tour started from Waterloo, the vast majority of the 325 miles was on Western Region lines.

A very well turned out No 30453 *King Arthur* headed the special to Reading via Weybridge, Virginia Water West Curve and Reading Old Junction, where it arrived a few minutes late, despite having attained 69 mph near Esher, to hand over to the famous No 3440 *City of Truro*. This locomotive was in superb external as well as mechanical condition, and achieved 79 mph during the journey to Bristol Temple Meads.

This was one of those tours which gradually got later and later due to various small things that, with

The famous No 3440 *City of Truro* heads the special near Bath Station *en route* to Bristol. Built in May 1903, the locomotive achieved fame in 1904 by attaining a claimed 102.3 mph down Wellington Bank in Somerset, being the first steam locomotive to reach 100 mph in Europe. It was retired to the York Railway Museum upon withdrawal in March 1931, where it remained until the mid-1950s when it was overhauled and returned to traffic, mainly on specials, although it did handle a few service trains.
Hugh Ballantyne

a little more attention to detail, could have been avoided.

At Bristol the 280 passengers were joined by a further 80 on the eight-coach train waiting in platform 14 and headed by Ivatt 2-6-2Ts Nos 41202 and 41203. The tour then travelled on the Bristol Harbour Branch, apparently being the first passenger train to do so since 1931, and then back on to the main line to Yatton. Here the special left the main line for Congresbury and Wrington, which was then the terminus of the Wrington Vale Light Railway. Time was lost on the run-round operation, and also because it was timed for 24 mph on a 10 mph restricted section, resulting in the return to Yatton being 47 minutes late.

The special continued down the main line to Highbridge via Weston-Super-Mare, then No 41202 headed the special on its own to Burnham and back to Highbridge, where No 41203 joined the train again. Departure for Bristol was now 57 minutes late, with both locomotives taking water at Yatton.

At Bristol the passengers returned to the original coaches; 2-6-2T No 5528 in lined green livery was now at the head of the train with *City of Truro*. Departure was 52 minutes late as the train headed along the North Somerset line to Radstock and across the Mendips to Frome.

At Westbury No 5528 was detached and took water before *City of Truro* was recoupled to the train and set off for Paddington where the train arrived 76 minutes late. The sight of *City of Truro* once again under the roof at Paddington after many years did much to placate the irritation of many of the passengers at the things that had gone wrong on the tour, through bad organisation on the part of the Western Region operators.

This picture was taken at Wrington, which was then the terminus of the branch off the North Somerset line from Congresbury to Blagdon. The Ivatt 2-6-2Ts are Nos 41202 and 41203, two of the ten members of the class built for the LMS, the rest being constructed for British Railways. No 41202 lasted until 1966, No 41203 until 1963. *Hugh Ballantyne*

A superb photograph, in fact the photographer's own favourite black and white picture, shows the special crossing Pensford Viaduct, situated about half way between Bristol and Radstock on the North Somerset line. The '4500' Class 2-6-2T No 5528 is resplendent in lined green livery which was applied to the class after 1958. Built in May 1928, it was withdrawn in November 1959. The train engine is, of course, *City of Truro*. What a colour slide this would have made if the 8 ASA Kodachrome of the time could have handled it. *Hugh Ballantyne*

Sunday 23 June 1957
Yorkshire Coast Rail Tours

This was the first RCTS rail tour that I had the pleasure of enjoying. It was jointly organised by the West Riding and Sheffield branches, and gave the passengers the opportunity to travel, in one day, over several lines which only had very sparse services, but which passed through beautiful countryside; the tour also provided some interesting motive power.

The tour started from Leeds and provided the opportunity to travel behind one of the famous Wilson Worsdell 'R' Class 4-4-0s, later to become the 'D20s'. At the date of the tour only four remained in service, all being moved to Alnmouth for the summer - No 62387 was due to be transferred

there after the tour, having been in store at Scarborough during the winter, and returned to traffic after a good clean on 31 May.

'D49/1' 4-4-0 No 62731 *Selkirkshire* took over the train from York Holgate to Alne. Here 'J71' No 68246 was waiting for the passengers to give a trip in open wagons and a four-wheeled van on the Easingwold Light Railway. From Alne No 62731 took the tour to Scarborough. Built in 1929, No 62731 survived until April 1959, based at York.

At Scarborough No 69881, believed to be the

Route map of the Yorkshire Coast Rail Tour. *RCTS*

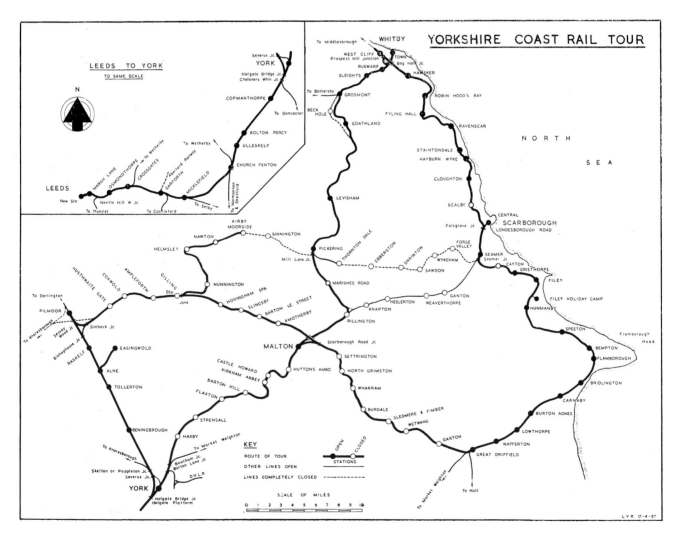

depot's only remaining active 'A8' 4-6-2T, joined No 62731 as pilot for the run to Whitby, with gradients as steep as 1 in 39. The 'A8' was apparently in good condition, having only travelled 40,000 miles since its last heavy repair at Darlington Works in November 1954, and the sight and sound from a window of the fourth coach can still be vividly remembered, as the locomotives worked flat out on the difficult route.

The 'D49/1' then continued for the trip back to York over the North Yorkshire Moors Line, the climb from Grosmont to the summit, now so well known to enthusiasts, taxing the locomotive to the limit. After many anxious moments the summit was reached, where a short stop was made for the locomotive to get its second wind.

Below Worsdell 'R' Class 4-4-0 No 62387 is seen in the sun at Leeds City station prior to backing on to the stock. *Gavin Morrison*

Right 'J71' No 68246, on hire from British Rail at York, was the Easingwold branch locomotive; built in July 1889, it survived until November 1958. The passengers are seen here boarding the train of open wagons at Alne. *Gavin Morrison*

SCHEDULE

M.	C.		Schedule
			a.m.
		LEEDS CITY (SOUTH) ......dep.	10-15
25	8	YORK, HOLGATE BRIDGE	
		arr.	10-50
		dep.	10-52
26	5	York Yard North ....pass	11-11
36	16	ALNE ....arr.	11-35
		dep.	11-45
38	53	EASINGWOLD ....arr.	11-55
			p.m.
		dep.	12-25
41	10	ALNE ....arr.	12-35
		dep.	12-45
46	2	PILMOOR ....dep.	1-10
57	6	GILLING ....arr.	1-32
		dep.	1-37
69	3	KIRBY MOORSIDE ....arr.	2-02
		dep.	2-12
81	0	GILLING ....arr.	2-38

M.	C.		Schedule
			p.m.
		GILLING ....dep.	2-48
93	25	Malton, Scarborough Road pass	3-18
99	34	WHARRAM ....arr.	3-37
		dep.	3-42
112	40	Driffield ....pass	4-18
123	75	BRIDLINGTON ....arr.	4-33
		dep.	4-38
146	38	SCARBOROUGH,	
		FALSGRAVE ....dep.	5-20
156	40	Ravenscar ....pass	5-48
167	63	WHITBY, WEST CLIFF .....arr.	6-15
		dep.	6-20
169	46	WHITBY TOWN ....arr.	6-26
		dep.	7-00
179	19	Goathland ....pass	7-21
204	64	Malton ....pass	8-10
225	76	YORK ....arr.	8-38
		dep.	8-45
251	40	LEEDS CITY (SOUTH) ......arr.	9-22

Above The special is shown at Easingwold. Passenger services ceased in November 1948. *Hugh Ballantyne*

Left The tour's schedule. *RCTS*

Below 'A8' No 69881 and the 'D49/1' after arriving at Whitby West Cliff station, before the train reversed down the gradient to Whitby Town. *Gavin Morrison*

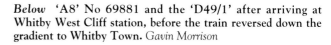

Right At Gilling 'D49/1' No 62731 *Selkirkshire* took water after a trip to Kirkby Moorside. This line closed to all traffic on 7 August 1964, although after 1953 it had mainly been used for ramblers' excursions and for trains conveying pupils to and from Ampleforth College at the start and end of terms. Until 1962 the line from Pilmoor through to Malton was used in the summer by through trains to Scarborough from the North East and beyond. Sometimes the trains were headed by 'Pacifics' and Class '40' diesels. Reversal took place at Malton.

The Malton to Driffield line lost its passenger service on 5 June 1950, but remained open until October 1958 for the freight traffic to Burdale Quarry. *Gavin Morrison*

27 April 1958 　　　Hertfordshire No 2

This tour of only 84 miles, which took nearly 7 hours to complete, was enjoyed by 360 participants. An eight-coach train headed by Class 'N7/4' No 69614, the beautifully cleaned Liverpool Street pilot, crewed by two Society members with a certain Mr R. Hardy in charge!

The tour departed from Fenchurch Street at midday and proceeded to South Tottenham via Stepney, the Cambridge line at Stratford and the new down goods line through Temple Mills Yard. Unfortunately No 69614 suffered a defective steam pipe joint in the smokebox and pressure was reduced to 100 lb; however, the tour struggled through to Junction Road where water was taken.

The train continued via Gospel Oak and Willesden to Harrow where '2P' 0-4-4T No 41901 took the party in a four-coach push-and-pull train to Stanmore, before returning to Watford Junction to join the main train.

No 69614 failed completely at Watford and No 41901 continued with its heavy load to St Albans where 'N7/5' 69632 was waiting to take the train on to Hatfield. The return journey was via Welwyn Garden City, Hertford North and East, Cheshunt, Churchbury, Lower Edmonton, Angel Road, Temple Mills, Stratford and Victoria Park to Broad Street, during which a 48-minute deficit at Harrow was converted to a 13-minute early arrival at Broad Street!

Left 'N7/4' 0-6-2T No 69614 was the favoured member of the class at Stratford Depot (30A), and was usually to be found at Liverpool Street station as the pilot engine, together with 0-6-0T Class 'J69/1' No 68619. The locomotive was fitted with a 'flowerpot' chimney and had been built at Stratford in December 1923; it lasted until December 1960. The photograph shows the immaculately turned out engine at Fenchurch Street, prior to departure. *Rodney Lissenden*

Above right The small class of ten 0-4-4Ts was introduced by the LMS in 1932 and is generally credited to William Stanier, but this was only because by coincidence they were constructed shortly after he had taken up office. They were actually designed by E. G. H. Lemon. Photographs of them seem to be scarce, but they did work the Watford-St Albans branch for some time, and in the early 1950s some were allocated to Gloucester, sub-shedded to Tewkesbury for working the one-coach service to Great Malvern via Upton-upon-Severn. No 41901 operated the special with a four-coach push-and-pull set between Watford and Stanmore, where it is seen in this photograph. *Rodney Lissenden*

Right Not quite up to the standard of cleanliness of No 69614, never the less 'N7/5' No 69632 was still commendably clean as can be seen in this picture of it ready to depart from St Albans. The locomotive was built in January 1926 and lasted until September 1962. *Rodney Lissenden*

4 October 1958   The Sapper

Two hundred passengers participated in this tour to the Longmoor Military Railway. LSWR Class 'T9' 4-4-0 No 30120 (now preserved) hauling four saloon coaches departed from Waterloo and ran via Epsom, Effingham Junction and Guildford to Liss. At Liss WD 2-8-0 No 400 *Sir Guy Williams* took over the train for the tour of the system. Unfortunately, because of a washout of an embankment the train could not traverse the complete Hollywater loop, but

the tour participants were able to visit the locomotive depot at Longmoor Down where seven Austerity 0-6-0STs were seen, in addition to No 600 *Gordon* and several diesels. Dean 0-6-0 No 2531, ex-WD195, used for re-railing made a sorry sight in the yard.

The tour continued through to Bordon where No 30120, which had worked light through the LMR system, was waiting to take the return train to Waterloo via Aldershot.

Below WD 2-8-0 No 400 *Sir Guy Williams* on arrival at Bordon having worked the tour through the LMR system from Liss. WD400 was originally No 7337 and was the engine hauling the munition train which exploded at Soham on 2 June 1944. *Rodney Lissenden*

Right In lovely evening light 'T9' No 30120 waits to leave Bordon for the run down the branch to Bentley then on to Waterloo via Aldershot. *Rodney Lissenden*

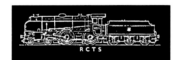

21 March 1959   London and North Kent

The Liverpool Street pilot, 'N7/4' No 69614, once more immaculately polished, was used again for the first part of this tour from Liverpool Street - on this occasion the locomotive performed without any problems! Having traversed the line to Bow Junction, the Carpenders Road curve, and joining the North London line at Victoria Park, the tour proceeded to Canonbury, where 'N2' 0-6-2T No 69504 took over for the run to Finsbury Park. The 'N2' worked to East Finchley and returned to Finsbury Park where 'J50' 0-6-0T No 68987 worked to King's Cross, through Snow Hill to Blackfriars.

The Southern turned out 'E1' 4-4-0 No 31507 to work the tour in Kent - unfortunately its cleanliness did not compare with its Eastern Region counterparts. The 'E1' took the seven-coach train with its 240 passengers to Gravesend West Street via Nunhead, Blackheath, Erith, the Bexley line to Hither Green, the curve to Chislehurst, Swanley and Fawkham.

The tour then returned to Hither Green where D8401 took over for the run to Liverpool Street via the East London line; this was the first use of a diesel-electric on a Society special.

Liverpool Street pilot No 69614 at Canonbury, having worked the first leg of the tour. *Rodney Lissenden*

Left 'N2' No 69504 suitably adorned with the Society headboard ready to leave Canonbury for East Finchley. *Rodney Lissenden*

Above right 'E1' 4-4-0 No 31507 about to run round the train at Gravesend West Street. *Rodney Lissenden*

2 May 1959

Brunel Centenarian and Plymouth District

To commemorate the centenary of the Royal Albert Bridge at Saltash and the death of its designer, Isambard Kingdom Brunel, the Society ran a special train from Paddington to Saltash on the actual anniversary of the opening of the bridge.

'Castle' Class 4-6-0 No 7001 *Sir James Milne* worked the special train of seven coaches and 250 tons for the complete journey to Saltash. A local tour had been arranged there, and '64xx' Class 0-6-0PT No 6420, sandwiched in the middle of four coaches, worked to Millbay, Friary and Plymstock.

LSWR '02' 0-4-4T No 30182 worked a two-coach LSWR push-and-pull 'gate' set from Plymstock to Turnchapel and into Admiralty property.

The train hauled by No 6420 was then re-boarded for the return trip to Plymouth via Yealmpton and the closed Laira goods yard.

The return journey to London was hauled appropriately by 'Castle' No 5069 *Isambard Kingdom Brunel* which ran well to Paddington, arriving about 10 minutes late. The tour covered 487 miles and at the time was probably the Society's longest.

Prior to departure, 'Castle' No 7001 *Sir James Milne*, at that time allocated to Old Oak Common depot, poses at the head of the seven-coach train under the vast roof at Paddington. The locomotive was later fitted with a double chimney in September 1960, just three years before its withdrawal. It was credited with running 838,604 miles between construction in May 1946 and its end at Cohen's scrapyard at Swansea. *Rodney Lissenden*

Sandwiched between two auto-coach units, Class '64xx' 0-6-0T No 6420 made a fine sight in the sunshine in its lined green livery; it was as late as January 1958 before the first member of the class received this livery. All 40 members of the class were built between 1932 and 1937 and were fitted for auto-train work. The train is seen standing at Plymouth Friary. *Rodney Lissenden*

Looking very smart in its BR lined black livery, ex-LSWR Class '02' 0-4-4T No 30192 stands at Turnchapel. Built in November 1890, the locomotive lasted until August 1961, being one of the last three members of the class to survive on the mainland; the class is best remembered for its association with the railways on the Isle of Wight. *Rodney Lissenden*

It was most appropriate that 'Castle' No 5069 *Isambard Kingdom Brunel* should be selected to return the tour to Paddington. The magnificent nameplate is well shown in this picture of the locomotive waiting to depart from Plymouth. Built in 1938, No 5069 is recorded as having covered 1,217,505 miles until its withdrawal at Swindon Works in February 1962. The double chimney was fitted in November 1958. Close examination of the photograph shows how few people travelling on the tour appeared to have cameras. *Rodney Lissenden*

3 October 1959   London River No 2

SE&CR Class 'H' 0-4-4T No 31193 was beauti-fully turned out by the staff of Tonbridge Depot for this tour. The train comprised three coaches filled with 155 passengers, and departed from Waterloo for Wimbledon via East Putney. The tour traversed the freight-only branch between Merton Park and Tooting Goods Depot, stopping at Merton Abbey for photographs, before returning to Wimbledon for water.

A fast run from Wimbledon to Peckham Rye was enjoyed before the train visited Deptford Wharf and the many spurs between New Cross Gate and Bricklayers Arms. The train then travelled to Blackheath and Angerstein Wharf before returning to Cannon Street.

South Eastern & Chatham 'H' Class 0-4-4T No 31193 was the locomotive used for this tour. Sixty-six were built between 1904 and 1915, and all but two survived into nationalisation. The last one to remain in traffic was No 31263 on the East Grinstead ser-vice on 4 January 1964; afterwards it passed into preservation.

In these two photographs the tour is seen (*below*) at Merton Abbey on the return journey from Tooting Goods Depot to Wimbledon, and (*above right*) at Deptford Wharf, an area now devoid of railways. Note that nearly every door of the three-coach set was open for passengers to jump down to inspect the area, something that would cause terrible trouble on today's railtours! *Both Rodney Lissenden*

Saturday 7 May 1960   J21 Rail Tour

This tour was organised in conjunction with the Stockton and Darlington Locomotive Society, and provided an opportunity to travel over Stainmore Summit, Belah Viaduct and Shap behind veteran North Eastern 'J21' No 65033. The tour was a sell-out, although it must be mentioned that the sturdy little 0-6-0 was restricted to three coaches. The driver decided, to the delight of the passengers if not the operating authorities, to tackle the climb to Shap Summit without a banker, and the locomotive made a steady ascent taking 13½ minutes.

It is interesting to note that this locomotive, as LNER No 876, was withdrawn in November 1939, but due to wartime pressures was reinstated, and then survived to become the last of the class, being withdrawn in April 1962. It then remained at Darlington Works for a further four years before being preserved, finding a permanent home at the North of England Open Air Museum at Beamish, where it has been frequently steamed.

Left Stops were made at Barnard Castle and Kirkby Stephen on the outward journey to Tebay, where 'J21' No 65033 was turned and prepared for the ascent of Shap Bank; the stock was shunted by Tebay Fowler 2-6-4T No 42396. Here we see the locomotive taking water at Barnard Castle. *Gavin Morrison*

Above No 42396 is seen with the stock on the North Eastern side of Tebay station. *Gavin Morrison*

Right The summit board at Stainmore. *Gavin Morrison*

Sunday 24 July 1960
Dukeries Rail Tour

I had limited knowledge of the South Yorkshire and Nottinghamshire branches and colliery lines, but this tour, while intended to improve my knowledge of the area, in fact confused me even further! Never the less 200 members enjoyed the 127-mile tour, albeit in poor weather conditions. Details of the tour are best shown by the schedule below.

SUNDAY 24th JULY, 1960
320 SPECIAL TRAIN

Class	A	Class	A
	a.m.		p.m.
Sheffield Vic.	10F35	Lincoln Central	2 33
Woodhouse	10 44	Pyewipe Junction	2 37
"	10 45	Tuxford West Junction	3 2
Woodhouse East Junction	10 47	Clipstone Junction	3 16
Beighton Stn. Junction	10 50	Welbeck Colliery Junction	3 21
Beighton Junction	10 53	" "	3 26
Foxlow Junction	11 5	Welbeck Colliery	3 39
Hall Lane Junction	11 8	"	3 51
Seymour Junction	11 12	Welbeck Colliery Junction	4 5
Glapwell Old Colliery	11 27	" "	4 16
	11 39	Shirebrook North	4 24
Seymour Junction	11 54	" "	4 29
"	12 3	Clowne South	4 44
Oxcroft Colliery No. 3	12 13	" "	4 49
Clowne & B.	12 16	Killamarsh Junction	5 3
"	12 21	Beighton Junction	5 7
Elmton & C.	12 27	Treeton Junction	5 13
Shirebrook West	12 35	Brightside Stn. Junction	5X24
Mansfield Town	12 42		SL
"	12 48	Mill Race Junction	5X27
Mansfield N.	12 50		ML
Mansfield E.	12 52	Sheffield Mid.	5 31
Mansfield Colliery Junction	12 56		
Rufford Junction	1 0		
Blidworth Junction	1 6		
Farnsfield	1 13		
Kirklington	1 18		
Southwell	1 24		
"	1 30		
Rolleston Junction	1 36		
Newark Castle	1 43		
G.N. Crossing	1 45		
Lincoln St. Marks	2 6		
" "	2 8		
Pelham Street	2 12		
" "	2 15		
Lincoln Central	2 18		

A. - Propel to Lincoln Central. F. - E.C.S. ex No. 10 Sidings, dep. 10†0 a.m.
STOCK. (B.S.O., 2 T.S.O., Cafcar, 2 T.S.O., B.S.O.
("R.C.T.S. - Lincoln Tour."

SPECIAL INSTRUCTIONS
Instructions for Working between Welbeck Colliery Sidings and Welbeck Colliery Junction.

The following instructions will apply during the time the Special (empty and loaded) passenger trains are occupying the lines on both outward and return journeys between Welbeck Colliery Junction and Welbeck Colliery Sidings :-

The train will be worked between Welbeck Colliery Junction and Welbeck Colliery Sidings with an engine at each end of the train and the driver of the engine at the rear of the train in both directions to carry the train staff.

Speed not to exceed 15 m.p.h.

All points which are not fitted with lock-bar and plunger, which have to be passed over in a facing direction must be clamped.

District Inspector to supervise the working.

Left The Special Traffic Notice for the Dukeries tour, showing some of the special instructions involved in running such trains. *RCTS*

Right After visiting Glapwell Old Colliery, Midland '4F' No 44590, of Staveley Barrow Hill Depot, and Ivatt 2-6-0 No 43145 prepare to leave Seymour Junction. *Gavin Morrison*

Right The complex route of the tour. *RCTS*

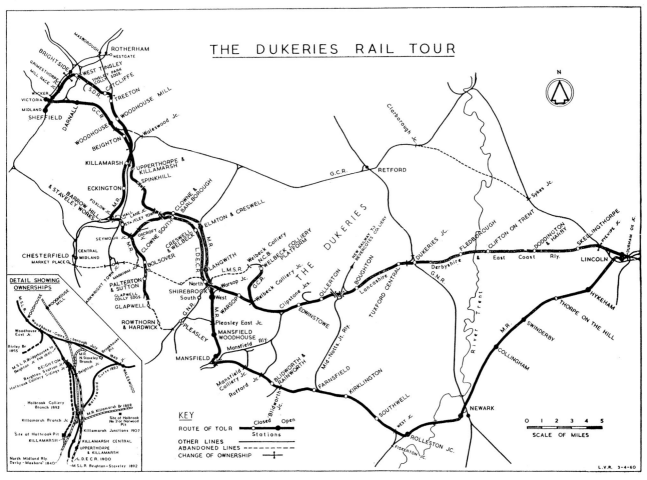

THE DUKERIES RAIL TOUR

KEY
ROUTE OF TO L R   Closed ○━━━● Open
                         Stations
OTHER LINES   ━━━━━━━
ABANDONED LINES   ----------
CHANGE OF OWNERSHIP ━━┼━━

DETAIL SHOWING
OWNERSHIPS

L.V.R. 3-4-60

Only 6 minutes were allowed at Mansfield Town for the Ivatt 2-6-0 to take water. Obviously this time was exceeded, judging by the number of participants who have left the train! *Gavin Morrison*

14 August 1960   The Greyhound

This tour started from Waterloo at 10.00 am and was powered by South Eastern & Chatham Railway Class 'L' 4-4-0 No 31768 hauling six coaches containing 240 passengers. The London & South Western main line was taken to Salisbury where LSWR Class 'T9' 4-4-0 No 30718 took over for the next leg of the journey to Weymouth via Yeovil Junction and Yeovil Pen Mill. The 'T9' performed well, reaching 69 mph near Gillingham and a minimum of 11 mph on the long 1 in 51 climb on the GWR line to Weymouth.

GWR 0-6-0PT No 3737 hauled the special over the Portland line to Easton with 240 passengers crowded into the three-coach train. On the return journey the Society gained another first when the police stopped the train on the causeway to search for escaped prisoners from the local prison! Fortunately they left empty handed and the journey resumed with numbers undiminished!

No 30718, assisted by a GWR 2-6-0 which banked the train out of Weymouth, hauled the tour back to Salisbury via Wareham, Broadstone and West Moors. From there No 31768 returned the train to Waterloo, but unfortunately failed to keep the 87-minute schedule for the 83-mile journey, arriving some 15 minutes late, although having attained a maximum speed of 70 mph.

SE&CR Class 'L' 4-4-0 31768 on arrival at Salisbury with the special from Waterloo. Note the driver receiving the congratulations of the tour participants for a good run. *Rodney Lissenden*

LSWR Class 'T9' 4-4-0 No 30718 runs round the train at Pen Mill having worked tender first from Yeovil Junction. *Rodney Lissenden*

GWR 0-6-0PT No 3737 takes water at Easton, which was closed to passengers in March 1952. *Rodney Lissenden*

Sunday 4 September 1960
Cumbrian Rail Tour

This was a very successful tour organised by the West Riding branch; its objective was not to cover rare or difficult routes, but to have an extremely scenic day out with a good variety of motive power. The highlight, of course, was having the Midland 'Compound' back in Leeds again, with a return trip over the Settle and Carlisle line. The last time 'Compounds' ran on the route was when the Holbeck locomotives were occasionally used to pilot the 'Thames-Clyde Express', and less frequently the 'Waverley', in the 1950s.

The journey to Carnforth with the 'Compound' was achieved without anything spectacular and arrival was on time, at which point Carnforth unrebuilt 'Patriot' No 45503 *The Royal Leicestershire Regiment* took over for the journey up the Cumbrian Coast to Workington. This proved to be a very unin-spiring performance, giving the passengers plenty of time to enjoy the fine scenery, resulting in a late arrival at Ravenglass, where a trip was taken on the narrow gauge line to Dalegarth. Three trains were run, headed by locomotives *River Irt*, *River Esk* and a diesel.

The tour arrived at Workington about half an hour down, and there the 'Patriot' gave way to two immaculately turned out Ivatt 2-6-0s, Nos 46442 and 46456 of Workington shed, to haul us over the steeply graded former Cockermouth, Keswick & Penrith line to Penrith.

At this point the whole character of the tour changed. These excellent little locomotives with enthusiastic crews really set about regaining time with a vengeance, giving a performance which must have ranked as one of the finest ever made over this route. I was fortunate to be travelling on the train engine, and the sound of the two locomotives blasting their way up to the summit around Troutbeck is never to be forgotten. The result of this remarkable run was that the half-hour arrears at Workington had been wiped out by the time we arrived at Penrith, where Midland 'Compound' No 1000 was waiting to take over for the journey to Leeds via the Settle and Carlisle line.

Little did the participants realise what a treat awaited them on the journey south. The driver was Jack Stone of Holbeck depot, Leeds; at that time he was in the London St Pancras link, so why he was on this duty was not clear, but the performance he gave between Appleby and Hellifield was remarkable. The 88 mph maximum through Settle was the fastest I had ever recorded on many trips.

Overleaf is a log timed by a friend, Jack Adamson, which I am sure will make interesting reading. (His notes tell me that the times between Hellifield and Skipton may be a little suspect.)

During a chat with a very cheerful driver back at Leeds, who had obviously enjoyed the trip as much as the passengers, he declared that the locomotive was in superb condition and rode very well indeed.

THE

RAILWAY CORRESPONDENCE AND TRAVEL SOCIETY

ITINERARY
of the
CUMBRIAN RAIL TOUR

LEEDS CITY NORTH · SKIPTON · CARNFORTH EAST · MILLOM
RAVENGLASS · DALEGARTH · WORKINGTON · PENRITH
CARLISLE · SKIPTON · LEEDS CITY NORTH

Sunday, 4th September, 1960

The cover of the tour brochure. *RCTS*

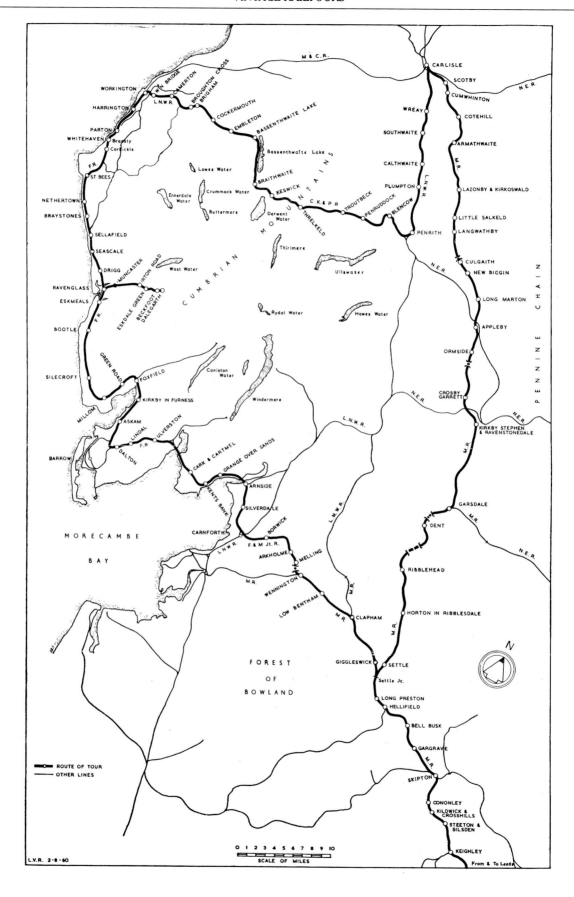

SCHEDULE

Mileage M. Ch.			a.m.	Mileage M. Ch.			p.m.
0. 0	LEEDS CITY NORTH	dep.	9-37	113.63	RAVENGLASS	dep.	2-35
10.38	Shipley Junction	pass	9-53	119.56	Sellafield	pass	2-44
26.14	SKIPTON	arr.	10-15 10·27	126.01	St. Bees	,,	2-57
	,,	dep.	10-18	128.20	Corkickle	,,	3-12
39.35	Settle Junction	pass	10-42	137.22	Workington	arr.	3-30
46.73	Clapham	,,	10-54		,,	dep.	3-38
63.53	Carnforth East	arr.	11-16	143.68	Brigham	pass	3-52
	,,	dep.	11-24	151.24	Bassenthwaite Lake	,,	4-10
72.65	Grange-over-Sands	pass	11-35	158.52	Keswick	,,	4-25
82.52	Ulverston	,,	11-47	162.07	Threlkeld	,,	4-36
87.62	Dalton Junction	,,	11-58	169.13	Penruddock	,,	4-53
				176.66	Penrith	arr.	5-06
			p.m.		,,	dep.	5-14
88.68	Park South	pass	12-05		Carlisle No. 13	pass	5-35
100.65	Millom	arr.	12-28	193.28	Carlisle No. 12	,,	5-39
	,,	dep.	12-33	194.19	Carlisle No. 7	,,	5-46
109.17	Bootle	pass	12-42		Durran Hill Sidings	,,	5-50
113.63	RAVENGLASS	arr.	12-50	209.02	Lazonby	,,	6-15
				229.29	Appleby West	,,	6-39
				241.74	Aisgill	,,	7-23
	RAVENGLASS	dep.	1-00	253.09	Blea Moor	,,	7-38
	DALEGARTH	arr.	1-35	267.09	Settle Junction	,,	7-54
				280.30	SKIPTON	arr.	8-16
					,,	dep.	8-20
	DALEGARTH	dep.	1-45	306.44	LEEDS CITY NORTH	arr.	9-02
	RAVENGLASS	arr.	2-25				

MR 'Compound' No 1000 - Driver Stone (Holbeck)
9 coaches, 295 tons nett?

Distance (m ch)		Time (min sec)	Speed (mph)
0.0	Petteril Bridge Junc (dep)	0.00	
	Durran Hill	2.32	20
1.8	Slotby	5.37	29
3.0	Cumwhinton	8.05	31/40
7.2	Mp 300	15.10	34/54
9.05	Armathwaite	17.26	55
12.15	Mp 295	21.05	48/54
14.55	Lazonby	23.38	60
17.45	Little Salkeld	26.35	55
18.85	Langwathby	28.35	20 (pws)
22.40	Culgaith	36.40	46
23.80	New Biggin	38.34	45/47
26.95	Long Marton	42.35	50
29.90	Appleby	46.28	45/57
32.35	Ormside	49.30	54
35.25	Griseburn	53.49	30
37.40	Crosby Garrett	59.36	40/46
40.55	Kirkby Stephen	62.20	35/30
43.90	Mallerstang	68.26	40
47.45	Ais Gill	74.30	30/56
50.50	Garsdale	80.00	1 (sigs)
53.75	Dent	86.27	51
55.85	Dent Head	88.37	58
	eased through tunnel		
58.65	Blea Moor box	91.48	63
59.90	Ribblehead	92.53	71/80
64.60	Horton	96.35	81/84
70.65	Settle	100.59	87/88 max
72.65	Settle Junction	102.26	70

Distance (m ch)		Time (min sec)	Speed (mph)
		103.27	
	(sig stop, 1 1/2 mins)		
		105.07	
74.65	Long Preston	109.05	35
75.90	Hellifield (arr)	113.20	
0.00	(dep)	0.00	
3.35	Bell Busk	-	60/65
6.25	Gargrave	9.22	68/70
		sigs	
10.00	Skipton (arr)	15.50	
	(dep)	0.00	
1.30	Snaygill	3.30	46
3.05	Cononley	5.42	52
4.25	Kildwick	7.12	55
6.15	Steeton	9.11	58
		sigs	10
9.20	Keighley	15.13	35
		17.25	
	(sig stop, 1/2 min)		
		17.55	
12.40	Bingley	24.47	20
13.55	Saltaire	28.28	42
14.45	Shipley Leeds Junction	30.15	25
17.55	Apperley Bridge	35.00	52
19.30	Calverley	36.50	56
20.50	Newlay	38.11	55
21.95	Kirkstall	39.46	54
23.45	Armley	41.36	42
		sig stops	
-	Holbeck	45.12	
		sig stops	
26.20	Leeds (arr)	52.56	

Left Midland 'Compound' No 1000 looking immaculate amongst the dirt and grime of Holbeck depot, just before it departed for Leeds City station to pick up the special. Just to the right-hand side of the water column can be seen the Shed Master of Holbeck at the time, Mr Ted Geeson, who did much for the West Riding branch over the years in selecting good locomotives for the tours, and making sure they were well cleaned.

The 'Compound' is now part of the National Railway Museum Collection, and although it has been used on steam specials, it has only ventured over the Settle and Carlisle line once, piloting 'Jubilee' *Leander* in terrible weather conditions. *Gavin Morrison*

Below Two very handsome locomotives seen side by side at Carnforth, where the 'Compound' was replaced by unrebuilt 'Patriot' No 45503. It was a terrible shame that one of these locomotives was not preserved, particularly as the last two, Nos 45543 *Home Guard* and 45550 were stored at Preston depot in good condition. *Gavin Morrison*

Passengers leave the train at Ravenglass, prior to crossing over to the narrow gauge line for a trip to Dalegarth. (*Inset*) Driver Jack Stone of Holbeck depot on the footplate of Midland 'Compound' No 1000. *Gavin Morrison*

Sunday 11 September 1960
East Midlander No 4 Rail Tour

This was the second weekend in succession that I had the pleasure of travelling behind the magnificent Midland 'Compound', so with memories of the exhaust of the loco climbing to Ais Gill the week before, and the maximum speed of 88 mph through Settle station, expectations were very high for this trip along the Great Central main line.

Departure was on time from Nottingham Victoria; the load was 242 tons net, with all the 336 seats sold. The performance was adequate if not spectacular, and arrival at Oxford was 4 minutes early.

Taking over at Oxford, 2-6-0 No 7317, in unlined green livery, was in superb condition, and gave an excellent performance, reaching 70 mph at Pangbourne, and 73 mph down the bank near Winchester, giving a

2 minutes early arrival at Eastleigh.

Standard 2-6-0 No 76006 was then provided to take the train to the Works, and plenty of time was available to visit both Works and depot, where a wide variety of motive power was on view.

The return journey was not designed for the benefit of the stop-watch brigade, and a very leisurely trip was made via Romsey and Andover, where a photographic stop was made. The special then ran over the former Midland & South Western Junction line to Swindon, where once again a visit to the Works and shed were organised.

'Compound' No 1000 was seen again, together with *City of Truro*. A leisurely trip back followed, with a maximum of 70 mph at Loughborough resulting in a 1 minute early arrival.

The schedule of the East Midlander. *RCTS*

'East Midlander' No.4 Rail Tour - Nottingham (Victoria) to Eastleigh Works & Swindon Works. -M950

Distance				Schedule	Actual
M.	Ch.			a.m.	a.m.
0	00	Nottingham Victoria	dep	8-25	
13	44	Loughborough Centrl.	pass	8-41	
23	35	Leicester Central	arr	8-52	
			dep	8-56	
36	42	Lutterworth	Pass	9-20	
43	25	Rugby Central	arr.	9-27	
			dep	9-28	
57	37	Woodford Halse	pass.	9-48	
59	18	Culworth Junction	pass	9-51	
67	35	Banbury Junction	pass	10-02	
68	48	Banbury General	arr	10-05	
			dep	10-07	
84	17	Cement Sidings	pass	10-30	
91	24	Oxford	arr.	10-40	
			dep.	10-50	
118	25	Reading West	arr.	11-25	
			dep	11-27	
119	21	Southcote Junction	pass	11-31	
132	70	Basingstoke	arr	11-53	
			dep	11-58	
				p.m.	p.m.
135	30	Worting Junction	pass	12-03	
149	47	Winchester Junc.	pass	12-21	
158	52	Eastleigh	arr	12-30	
			dep	12-42	
-	-	Eastleigh Works	arr.	12-47	
			dep	2-10	
158	52	Eastleigh	pass	2-15	
165	78	Romsey	pass	2-30	
168	78	Kimbridge Junc.	pass	2-35	
183	21	Andover	arr	3-05	
			dep	3-15	
216	32	Swindon Town	arr	4-25	
			dep	4-30	
-	-	Swindon Works	arr	4-48	
			dep	6-55	

Distance				Schedule	Actual
M.	Ch.			p.m.	p.m.
219	27	Swindon Junction	arr.	7-00	
			dep	7-05	
240	09	Steventon	pass	7-32	
253	17	Oxford	arr	7-58	
			dep	8-01	
260	24	Cement Sidings	pass	8-12	
275	73	Banbury General	arr	8-34	
			dep	8-38	
277	06	Banbury Junction	pass	8-41	
285	23	Culworth Junction	pass	8-53	
287	04	Woodford Halse	pass	8-56	
301	16	Rugby Central	arr	9-17	
			dep	9-20	
307	79	Lutterworth	pass	9-30	
321	06	Leicester Central	arr	9-43	
			dep	9-47	
330	77	Loughborough Cent.	pass	10-00	
344	41	Nottingham Victoria	arr	10-17	

Note:- The mileage from Leicester returning to Leicester is 297 miles 51 chains

The mileage from Rugby returning to Rugby is 257 miles 71 chains

The mileage from Reading West returning to Oxford is 134 miles 72 chains.

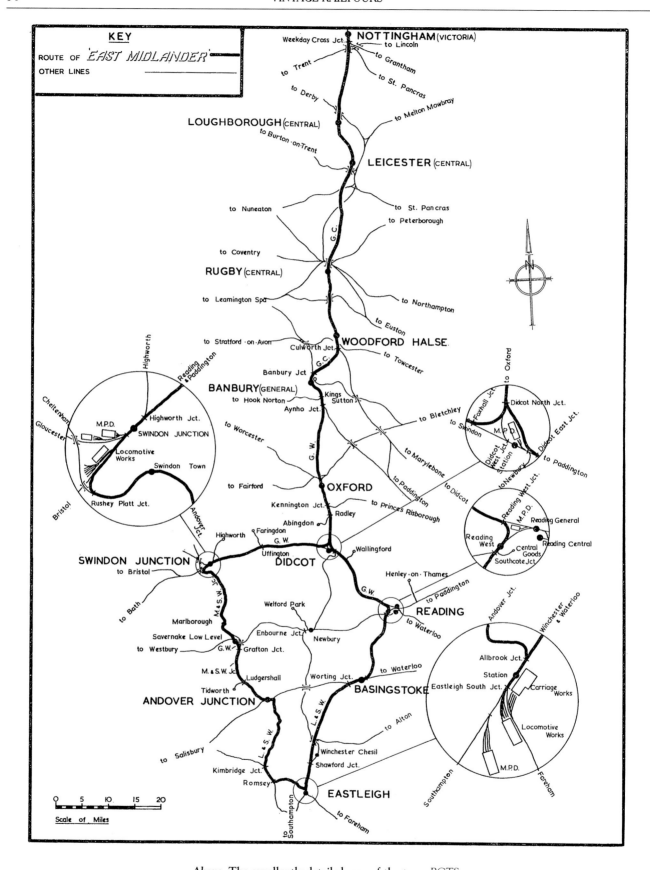

KEY
ROUTE OF *'EAST MIDLANDER'*
OTHER LINES

Above The excellently detailed map of the tour. *RCTS*

Right Midland 'Compound' No 1000 and its train at Nottingham Victoria just prior to departure. *Gavin Morrison*

Left A change of motive power took place at Oxford and gave us the rare opportunity to photograph the 'Compound' alongside ex-works Great Western '43xx' Class No 7317. The 'Compound' then ran light engine to Swindon ready for the return trip. *Gavin Morrison*

Below left A general view at Eastleigh station, with Standard '4MT' 2-6-0 No 76006 ready to take the special to the Works. Rebuilt 'Battle of Britain' No 34090 *Sir Eustace Missenden Southern Railway* awaits departure on a down train. Note the impressive Southern Railway notice in front of No 76006. *Gavin Morrison*

Above The special at Andover Junction station. The London & South Western main lines are on the right. *Gavin Morrison*

Below Of particular interest on the Swindon Works scrap line was the Brown-Boveri gas turbine locomotive No 18000. It entered service in 1950, and was withdrawn not long after our visit, in December 1960.

Sunday 9 July 1961   Borders Rail Tour

This tour must surely rank as one of the finest organised by the West Riding branch. Just consider what it offered:

- six different locomotives
- the first Stanier 'Pacific' over the Settle and Carlisle line northwards for many years (was it a first?)
- a record climb from Settle Junction to Blea Moor
- the Settle-Carlisle, the Waverley route, and a fast run down the East Coast Main Line
- over 400 miles
- the preserved North British *Glen Douglas*
- superb scenery around the Borders

The map reproduced opposite tells it all, together with the journey schedule.

This was a tour that I particularly remember as it was the first time I attempted to follow, or some would say chase, the train. Starting at Newcastleton, I had to finish at Tweedmouth as I was on holiday at North Berwick at the time. I have always regretted not being on the train from Leeds to Carlisle.

Below is the log of the performance of No 46247 *City of Liverpool* from Hellifield to Blea Moor, with ten coaches for 365 tons tare. The train was timed by Mr B. J. Hastings.

Miles		Time (min sec)	Speed (mph)
0.00	Hellifield	0.00	
1.25	Long Preston	2.35	
3.25	Settle Junction	4.31	71
5.25	Settle	6.20	61
7.00	Stainforth Sidings	8.04	60
9.60	Helworth Bridge	10.48	56/60
11.25	Horton	12.25	60
13.60	Selside signal box	14.50	59
16.00	Ribblehead	17.18	56/58
17.25	Blea Moor	18.38	56

The overall average from Leeds to Carlisle gave a net time of 113.5 minutes for the 112.1 miles.

Thompson 'B1s' Nos 61290 and 61242 *Alexander Reith Gray* took over at Carlisle for the trip on the Waverley route to Hawick. The locomotives did not, however, perform well, with speed dropping to 26 mph on the climb past Steele Road to Whitrope Summit, giving a 10 minutes late arrival at Hawick.

The immaculate preserved North British 4-4-0 *Glen Douglas* and 'J37' No 64624, also well cleaned, took over from Hawick for the tour around the Border Country, which eventually resulted in a 24 minutes late arrival at Tweedmouth.

Here immaculate 'A1' No 60143 *Sir Walter Scott*, a most appropriate choice for this tour, backed on to the train for a brisk run to Newcastle; many miles were covered at 75 mph, with a maximum of 80 mph near Morpeth.

At Newcastle the 'A1' gave way to one of the well-known quartet of Neville Hill depot's 'A3s', No 60074 *Harvester*, which continued to regain time. By the time Leeds was reached, via Ripon, at the end of this 408-mile tour (in fact 405 miles, as the Bishop Auckland route was not taken after Durham) the passengers had enjoyed 12 hours of superb locomotive performance, and beautiful Border Country scenery on a fine sunny day.

THE
RAILWAY CORRESPONDENCE AND
TRAVEL SOCIETY

ITINERARY

of the

BORDERS RAIL TOUR

LEEDS (CITY) - SKIPTON - AIS GILL - CARLISLE (GOODS LINES) - HAWICK
ST. BOSWELLS - GREENLAW - ROXBURGH - JEDBURGH - COLDSTREAM
TWEEDMOUTH - NEWCASTLE - DURHAM - BISHOP AUCKLAND
DARLINGTON - NORTHALLERTON - RIPON - HARROGATE
ARTHINGTON - LEEDS (CITY)

Sunday, 9th July, 1961

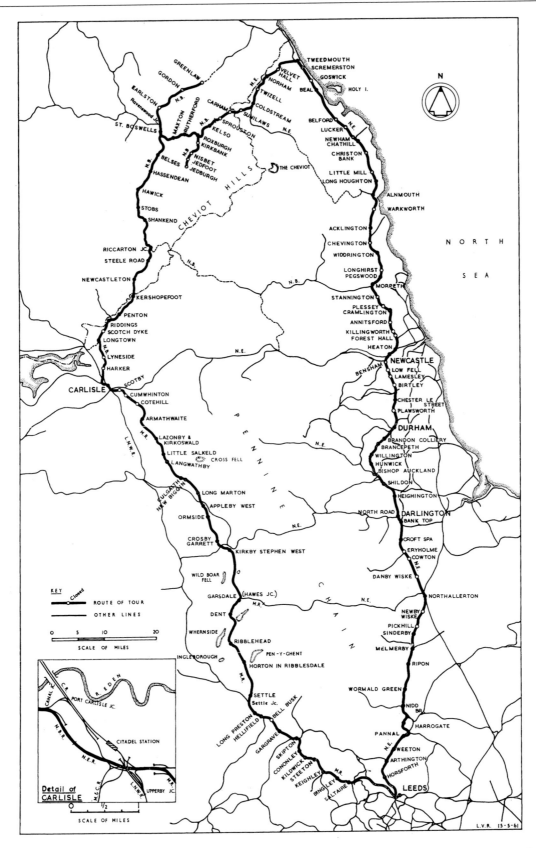

It is sad to reflect how much of this tour ran on track which has since vanished from the railway network, but at least the beautiful Leaderfoot Viaduct still exists, and it has just been announced as I write these notes that *Glen Douglas* is to be returned to working order for use on the West Highland line.

SCHEDULE

Mileage M. Ch.			Schedule a.m.
0.00	LEEDS CITY (SOUTH)	dep.	9-50
10.57	SHIPLEY (LEEDS JCT.)	pass	10-05
17.00	KEIGHLEY	pass	10-12
25.01	SNAYGILL	pass	10-20
26.15	SKIPTON STN.	pass	10-22
36.15	HELLIFIELD	pass	10-35
39.35	SETTLE JCT.	pass	10-38
53.35	BLEA MOOR	pass	10-56
64.50	AIS GILL	pass	11-08
82.15	APPLEBY WEST	pass	11-22
111.35	DURRAN HILL S.S.	pass	11-46
112.25	PETTERIL BRIDGE JCT.	arr.	11L48
			Noon
		dep.	12L00
			p.m.
112.48	CARLISLE No. 7	pass	12-02
112.71	CARLISLE No. 10	pass	12-06
113.10	CARLISLE No. 11	pass	12-08
114.05	CARLISLE No. 3	pass	12-13
114.16	CANAL JCT.	pass	12-15
122.35	LONGTOWN JCT.	pass	12-24
126.72	RIDDINGS JCT.	pass	12-29
137.07	NEWCASTLETON	pass	12-42
145.16	RICCARTON JCT.	pass	12-58
147.29	WHITROPE SDG.	pass	1-03
158.17	HAWICK	arr.	1L19
		dep.	1L29
170.39	ST. BOSWELLS	pass	1-47
—	RAVENSWOOD JCT.	pass	1-50
185.00	GREENLAW	arr.	2-20
		dep.	2-32
—	RAVENSWOOD JCT.	pass	3-02
199.41	ST. BOSWELLS	arr.	3-05
		dep.	3-10

Mileage M. Ch.			Schedule p.m.
199.63	KELSO JCT.	pass	3-11
208.00	ROXBURGH	pass	3-25
215.00	JEDBURGH	arr.	3-48
		dep.	4-00
221.60	ROXBURGH JCT.	arr.	4-25
		dep.	4-35
224.60	KELSO	pass	4-41
229.26	CARHAM	pass	4-48
234.52	COLDSTREAM	pass	4-58
247.08	TWEEDMOUTH	arr.	5L21
		dep.	5L31
261.21	BELFORD	pass	5-47
278.04	ALNMOUTH	pass	6-03
296.23	MORPETH	pass	6-20
312.73	NEWCASTLE	arr.	6L43
		dep.	6L51
313.41	KING EDWARD BRIDGE	pass	6-54
327.78	DURHAM	pass	7-11
335.14	WILLINGTON	pass	7-26
339.07	BISHOP AUCKLAND	pass	7-34
342.01	SHILDON	pass	7-41
351.03	DARLINGTON	arr.	7-58
		dep.	8-00
365.17	NORTHALLERTON	pass	8-15
373.15	SINDERBY	pass	8-24
379.00	RIPON	pass	8-32
390.37	HARROGATE	pass	8-48
399.36	ARTHINGTON	pass	9-01
408.58	LEEDS CITY (SOUTH)	arr.	9-20

The special appears to be going well in this picture taken just before Newcastleton. The leading locomotive, No 61242 *Alexander Reith Gray*, has 'Kittybrewster' painted on the buffer beam, making it an unusual locomotive for this route. The other 'B1', No 61290, was allocated to Carlisle Canal shed. *Gavin Morrison*

The superb combination of North British motive power, preserved 'Glen' No 256 *Glen Douglas* (BR number 62469) and 'J37' No 64624 of St Margaret's depot, leaves Hawick for a journey to Greenlaw. The entrance to the small motive power depot was just behind the locomotives. *Gavin Morrison*

The special is next seen ready to leave Greenlaw to return to St Boswells. Greenlaw was at that time the terminus of the line which originally went to Duns, and eventually joined the East Coast Main Line near Reston. The line lost its passenger service on 12 August 1948, following the terrible Border floods. The section from Reston to Duns closed on 7 November 1966, passenger services having been withdrawn on 10 September 1951. *Gavin Morrison*

The special arrives back at Roxburgh having travelled down the branch to Jedburgh. The locomotives then ran round the train and headed to Tweedmouth via Coldstream. 'J37' No 64624 was withdrawn in January 1966. *Gavin Morrison*

Left The Borders Rail Tour crossing what must be one of the most elegant viaducts in the country, at Leaderfoot, situated on the now closed line to Greenlaw, near the former junction with the Waverley route. *Gavin Morrison*

Right The special leaves Tweedmouth, and sets off for a lively run to Newcastle behind 'A1' No 60143 *Sir Walter Scott*. The 'Pacific' was a Heaton locomotive in 1961, and lasted until May 1964; although being allocated to Tweedmouth in September 1962, it finished its days at York. *Gavin Morrison*

10 September 1961 MSWJR

The closure of the whole of the former Midland & South Western Junction route, except for short sections for freight services only, provided the occasion for this tour.

Ex-GWR '43xx' 2-6-0 No 5306 left Swindon hauling eight coaches and over 250 passengers for Andover via Swindon Town, Marlborough, Savernake and Ludgershall. After some problems with point clearance at Andover, No 5306 was turned and returned to Cheltenham Spa (St James), having passed through some lovely countryside stopping at Cricklade, Cirencester and Foss Cross.

At Cheltenham No 5306 was turned again and gave a spirited performance on its return journey to Swindon via Gloucester and Stroud.

Ex-GWR '43xx' 2-6-0 No 5306 uncouples from the train at Andover to run round before the return run to Cheltenham (St James) during this complete tour of the former Midland & South Western Junction Railway. *Rodney Lissenden*

Saturday 20 January 1962
The Stainmore Limited

This tour was organised by the North Eastern branch. The 400 passengers assembled at Darlington Bank Top station on a dismal January morning to pay their last respects to the famous Stainmore line, at 1,370 ft the highest summit in England, and made even more famous by the remarkable British Transport Films' *Snowdrift at Bleath Ghyll*, which most enthusiasts must have seen many times.

The special pulled out on time headed by BR Standard '3MT' No 77003 and '4MT' No 76049, both well cleaned for the occasion. Although the tour mileage was under 200 miles, it was to be a 14-hour trip, so the special could be the last train to work over the line. The nine-coach train headed out to Shildon via the branch to West Auckland, then over the fell to Barnard Castle where water was taken.

The train then set off for Stainmore Summit where a stop was made. The weather started to improve before the decent to Kirkby Stephen, which involved crossing the famous Belah Viaduct, 1,047 feet long and 196 feet high, the highest in England. It was an impressive structure, as can be seen in the accompanying photograph, and although one was able to get to it by car, there were, if I remember, seven farm gates to open and close before the photographic location was reached. Myself and two friends were the only people present to witness the passing of the special, and I very much doubt if anybody turned out at 10.30 pm that January night to see the return working.

The defunct locomotive shed at Kirkby Stephen was inspected by many passengers while the locomotives took water ready for the last run to Tebay, where water was again taken before the train returned to Kirkby Stephen.

At this point the light started to fade and I returned home after having taken the pictures I wanted. The tour passengers, however, still had another eight hours to go before arrival back at Darlington.

On the return trip the train experienced minor problems caused by a DMU on the West Coast Main Line between Carlisle and Penrith, and a single-line tablet failure was encountered at Clifton Moor. At Appleby the train was greeted by the Mayor, together with the usual big crowd that gathered in the 1950s and 1960s to see last trains, and of course there were detonators laid on the track.

Kirkby Stephen had the town band on the platform playing 'Will ye no come back again' and the final ascent to Stainmore Summit commenced 24 minutes late to more exploding detonators.

As had happened on so many previous occasions, the difficult climb proved too much for the locomotives, and a stop for a 'blow up' had to be made before the summit was reached, the still night being disturbed by much whistling as the train passed Barras and the summit for the final time.

Eventually Barnard Castle was reached 45 minutes late, and thus another famous railway route passed into the history books.

The tour eventually arrived back at Darlington a few minutes before midnight. It was quite a day out for the middle of January, and excellent value for £1 10s 0d!

CHRONOLOGY OF THE LINE.

Darlington — Barnard Castle
Opened 8th July, 1856.

Barnard Castle — Barras
Opened 26th March, 1861.

Barras — Tebay
Opened 4th July, 1861.

Kirkby Stephen — Clifton and Lowther
Opened 7th June, 1862.

West Auckland — Barnard Castle
Opened 1st August, 1863.

Middleton-in-Teesdale Branch.
Opened 12th May, 1868.

NOTES.

1. In the Schedule overleaf, notes are used to signify the following:-

    Note "L" - Stop for locomotive purposes only; passengers are requested NOT to leave the train.

    Note "P" - Photographic stop; passengers may leave the train, but are requested not to delay its departure.

2. The stop at Stainmore Summit on the outward journey is NOT, at the time of writing, a photographic stop, and passengers are requested NOT to leave the train: an announcement will, however, be made about this before the train reaches Stainmore.

3. Passengers using the Buffet Car are requested not to remain in the seats any longer than is necessary, so that other passengers may use the Buffet Car facilities.

4. Arrangements have been made for passengers to retain their tickets at the end of the Tour.

5. British Railways have been requested to hold the 11.15 p.m. departure to Saltburn if the special train is running late.

6. For passengers staying overnight in Darlington, the following visits have been arranged for Sunday, 21.1.62:

    Darlington Shed: 10.00 a.m. (maximum 25)
    do.   10.30 a.m.   "
    Darlington Works: 11.00 a.m. (maximum 50)
    Notification should be made to any Committee member.

SCHEDULE.

Mileage M. Ch.			a.m.
00. 00	DARLINGTON (BANK TOP)	dep.	10.46
08. 76	Shildon South	pass.	11.07
10. 39	Shildon North	pass.	11.12
	Fieldens Bridge	pass.	11.18
12. 04	West Auckland	pass.	11.22
21. 62	Forth Burn	pass.	11.42
22. 77	Coal Road	pass.	11.45
24. 16	BARNARD CASTLE	arr.	11P48
			p.m.
37. 52	STAINMORE SUMMIT	dep.	12.05
		arr.	12.32
		dep.	12.37
46. 70	KIRKBY STEPHEN EAST	arr.	1.05
	"	dep.	1.15
52. 56	RAVENSTONEDALE	arr.	1P28
	"	dep.	1.38
58. 58	TEBAY	arr.	1.50
	"	dep.	2.10
70. 46	KIRKBY STEPHEN EAST	arr.	2.31
	"	dep.	2.50
81. 73	APPLEBY JUNC. GROUND FRAME	arr.	3L15
	" " " "	dep.	3L25
82. 29	APPLEBY WEST	arr.	3.30
	"	dep.	3.46
82. 65	APPLEBY JUNC. GROUND FRAME	arr.	3L51
	" " " "	dep.	3L53
92. 56	CLIFTON MOOR	arr.	4P11
	"	dep.	4.25
96. 33	PENRITH	arr.	4.33
	"	dep.	4.43
114. 13	CARLISLE	arr.	5.05
00. 00	"	dep.	8.13
17. 60	PENRITH	arr.	8L44
	"	dep.	8L46
42. 69	KIRKBY STEPHEN EAST	arr.	9L34
	"	dep.	9L39
52. 07	Stainmore Summit	pass.	10.00
65. 43	BARNARD CASTLE	arr.	10.20
		dep.	10.25
67. 39	Broomielaw	pass.	10.30
71. 11	Winston	pass.	10.37
82. 12	DARLINGTON (BANK TOP)	arr.	11.00

Left The Stainmore Limited going well through Bowes before really getting into the long climb to the 1,370-foot Stainmore Summit. *Gavin Morrison*

Below The special crossing the famous Belah Viaduct, built in 1859 - the maximum height above the ground was 196 feet, and it was 1,047 feet long. The section of line between Barras and Tebay was opened on 4 July 1861. After closure the viaduct was completely dismantled. *Gavin Morrison*

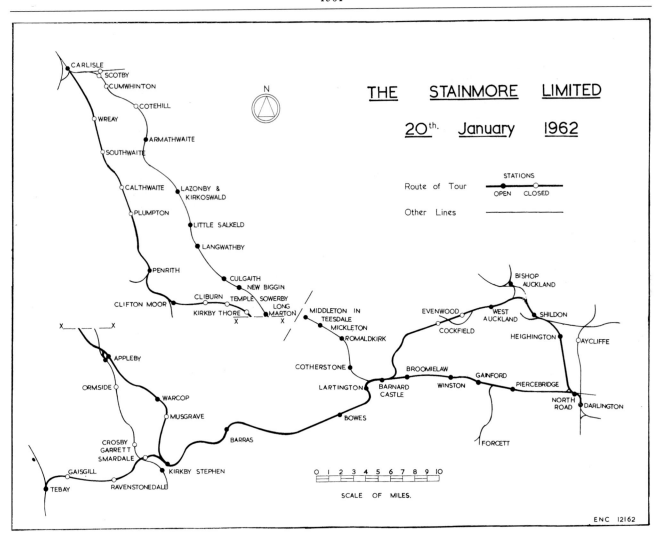

THE STAINMORE LIMITED
20th. January 1962

	STATIONS
Route of Tour	OPEN ——●——○—— CLOSED
Other Lines	———————

ENC 12162

Left The Stainmore Limited was the last train to leave Kirkby Stephen for Tebay. The Class '4' 2-6-0s were the largest locomotives allowed over the line, the regular motive in the latter years being usually the '2MT' 2-6-2T 82000 and '2MT' 78000 Standard classes, although the summer extras from the North East to Blackpool were regularly double-headed by the Standard '4MT' 76000 locomotives. *Gavin Morrison*

Right The special, with the leading locomotive blowing off, approaches Tebay from Kirkby Stephen. *Gavin Morrison*

31 March 1962
Great Eastern Commemorative

This was a tour arranged to commemorate the passing of steam on the former Great Eastern lines. 'Britannia' 4-6-2 No 70003 *John Bunyan*, cleaned by March depot, set off from Liverpool Street at 9.10 am for Ipswich; 292 passengers were carried in a six-coach train. No 70003 performed well, topping Brentwood bank at 59 mph and arriving at Ipswich 5 minutes early, having covered the 68.7 miles in 70 minutes.

The tour then proceeded to Norwich, when Hunslet 0-6-0 diesel No 11168 was attached to draw the train to Trowse Upper Junction in order that the 'Britannia' could proceed to Norwich Thorpe.

'J17' 0-6-0 No 65567 was attached for the run to Dereham via Wymondham, then on to County School and Foulsham. The train returned to Thetford via Swaffham. There *John Bunyan* was watered ready to return the tour to Liverpool Street.

Below 'Britannia' 4-6-2 No 70003 *John Bunyan* entered traffic on Great Eastern main line services in March 1951. After only 16 years' service it was finally withdrawn, like so many other members of the class, from Kingmoor depot at Carlisle, where for several years it had been employed on freight and secondary passenger duties. Immaculately cleaned for the tour, it is seen here near Thetford. *Rodney Lissenden*

Above right 'J17' 0-6-0 No 65567 approaches Thetford after visits to Dereham, County School and Swaffham. Built in May 1905 and superheated in September 1923, it lasted for only another five months after the tour. It was not the last of the class to be withdrawn, but was selected as the most suitable example when it was decided to retain a 'J17' for preservation. It was repainted at Doncaster Works as LNER No 1217E, and is now part of the National Collection. *Rodney Lissenden*

Sunday 13 May 1962
The East Midlander No 5

The East Midland branch of the RCTS had earned an excellent reputation for its tours, and the 360 members and friends who departed from Nottingham Victoria at 8.35 am in the eight coaches of this special were in for a good day out, with 300 miles behind the unusual double-headed combination of Midland '2P' No 40646 and 'Schools' 4-4-0 No 30925 *Cheltenham* of Basingstoke.

The route was down the Great Central to Staveley, and the train arrived at Sheffield Darnell 6 minutes early. From there the Masborough line was taken to Tinsley Junction, then the Great Central

Barnsley branch, already closed to passenger traffic, and on to Lancashire & Yorkshire tracks to Barnsley Exchange.

The two locomotives took water at Barnsley Jumble Lane, then headed to Horbury Junction and the L&Y route to Goose Hill at Normanton, before progressing east to Church Fenton, where the Wetherby Branch was taken. Reversal took place at Wetherby Town, and the locomotives worked tender first to Starbeck.

From there the Ripon to Northallerton line was the route taken to Darlington, where ex-works

Austerity 2-8-0 No 90348 took over for the short trip to the Works, followed by a visit to the shed.

The highlight of the tour was, however, yet to come, on the famous East Coast Main Line 'racing ground', and the details of the journey to York were as follows, as reported in the *Railway Observer*.

'The return journey commenced from Bank Top station at 4.12 pm after suitable wagers had been made about the probable running time over the famous racing ground. A thrilling run to York was made in 39 minutes 21 seconds for the 44.1 miles with a maximum of $83\frac{1}{2}$ mph sustained for three miles - 60 mph was reached only three miles from Darlington, 70 mph in six miles, and altogether some twelve miles were covered at over 80 mph! Arrival at York was six minutes early. The pessimists were duly relieved of their money, and many passengers rushed forward to congratulate the crews.'

The performance was exceptional, especially as the Midland '2P' had been withdrawn from service the day before; the boiler was life expired, but the locomotive was granted a one-off reprieve for the tour.

I heard it said by some of the participants that the

Miles		Schedule	Actual	Speed
00.00	Darlington			
	Bank Top		00.00	
02.55	Croft Spa		04.16	60
05.15	Eryholme		06.45	
				79
14.15	Northallerton	16	14.05	
				82
21.90	Thirsk	23	20.11	
				$83\frac{1}{2}$
28.00	Pilmoor		25.10	
32.90	Alne		28.20	76
38.55	Beningborough		32.48	
42.50	Skelton		36.06	$77\frac{1}{2}$
44.10	York	45	39.21	

Average speed 67.2 mph. 12 miles covered at over 80 mph.

'Schools' was virtually pushing the '2P' as well as hauling the 260-ton load, but that is speculation.

From York the return route was by Knottingley and on to Newark, where the Bottesford branch was taken, and so back to Nottingham Victoria at 9.41 pm.

Below A view taken from the rear of *Cheltenham* at York, showing that there was still plenty of coal left in the tender for the return trip to Nottingham. The footplate of the 'Schools' seems well filled with young enthusiasts! *Gavin Morrison*

Above right The locomotives simmer gently at York after their epic dash along the famous 'racing ground' from Darlington to York. *Gavin Morrison*

2 & 3 June 1962   The Aberdeen Flyer

This memorable tour was organised by the joint committee of the RCTS and the Stephenson Locomotive Society. The main reason for the mammoth outing was to celebrate, if that is the correct way of expressing it, the last non-stop run by steam from King's Cross to Edinburgh.

King's Cross 'Top Shed' appropriately selected *Mallard* for the occasion, and with eight coaches behind the tender she departed promptly at 8.00 am, being allowed 6 hr 25 min for the 393 miles to Waverley.

Everything went exactly to plan, with a crew change-over north of York, until the special reached Chathill, just south of Berwick, and the non-stop run was ruined by a hot axle-box on a freight ahead. This was a major disappointment to the 250 passengers, particularly since it was so far into the journey that the crew had no chance, in spite of some fine running, to get to the capital on time, so a 20 minutes late arrival was recorded.

Mallard was replaced at Edinburgh Waverley by one of Haymarket's (64B) old faithfuls, 'A4' No 60004 *William Whitelaw*. Now with only seven coaches, as the Kitchen car had been removed, the train departed at 2.56 pm, and was due at Aberdeen at 6.8 pm. The customary water stop was made at Dundee, and with some excellent running the special rolled into the 'Granite City' some 5 minutes early.

With a couple of hours to spare before the evening trip, many passengers refreshed themselves in the local cafes before returning to board five coaches for a trip to Old Meldrum. Preserved Great North of Scotland 4-4-0 *Gordon Highlander* was the most appropriate motive power, departure being from Aberdeen Waterloo goods station. The locomotive stalled on slippery rails near Kittybrewster, but managed to get going again.

At Inverurie 'J36' No 65345 attached itself to the rear for the trip to Old Meldrum and back, and then

the 'J36' headed the special back to Aberdeen.

The two locomotives selected for the return journey via the West Coast route were 'Princess Royal' 'Pacifics' Nos 46200 and 46201, and as it turned out this trip was really the 'swan song' for this famous class.

Green liveried No 46201 *Princess Elizabeth*, now happily preserved and used regularly on main-line outings, departed promptly at 11.00 pm. It could have taken a real optimist to believe that on a Saturday night/Sunday morning, with all the electrification and other engineering works in progress, that the special would arrive on time, and so it proved. *Princess Elizabeth* ran well but had to make three apparently unscheduled water stops during the night, at Forfar, Stirling and Beattock Summit, resulting in a 60 minutes late arrival at Carlisle.

For those that witnessed the change-over in the early hours of the morning, the two red and green locomotives must have made a memorable sight. By Crewe the arrears were up to 104 minutes, and No 46200 left with a load of 14 coaches for Euston. Further delays occurred due to engineering work and *Princess Royal* eventually pulled up at the buffer stops at Euston 178 minutes late.

In spite of the disappointing performance on the return journey, it was a memorable, if not somewhat exhausting, 37-hour trip!

Left 'Top Shed' had appropriately selected 'Mallard' for the East Coast Main Line non-stop attempt, and as can be seen from this photograph at King's Cross station, the 'A4' was turned out in superb external condition. *Hugh Ballantyne*

Below The elegant Great North of Scotland 4-4-0 *Gordon Highlander* is seen on home territory at Aberdeen Waterloo, prior to leaving on the evening trip to Old Meldrum. No 49 was built in October 1920 by the North British Locomotive Co, although its looks would suggest a much earlier date. It was finally withdrawn from BR stock in June 1958; in July it was repainted in the pre-Heywood green livery of the old company and then ran specials over a wide area of Scotland before being placed in the Glasgow Transport Museum. *Hugh Ballantyne*

Looking superb in its red livery, No 46200 *Princess Royal* makes an unscheduled stop at Watford near the end of the journey up the West Coast Main Line. It was reported that the stop was due to the locomotive being short of steam. No 46200 continued in service until December of 1962, being the last of the class to be withdrawn. It remained at Kingmoor depot for some time before being moved to Upperby depot, where it stayed in the hope that it would be preserved, but this was not to be. *Hugh Ballantyne*

Sunday 22 May 1962
Festiniog Scenic Rail Tour

The majority of the tours organised by the West Riding branch over the years tended to head north, but on this occasion it was decided to visit the Festiniog Railway.

On the face of it this tour looked as if it would present no problems. There was a great variety of motive power, which included Stanier 'Pacific' No 46200 *Princess Royal* again, plus excellent scenery, but as things turned out there were difficulties.

Two portions of the tour were run, one from Bradford Exchange and the other from Leeds Central, and they should have departed simultaneously, being due to combine at Halifax. The Bradford portion arrived as scheduled headed by local 'Royal Scot' No 46145 *The Duke of Wellington's Regiment*, but the Leeds portion, headed by 'Jubilee' 4-6-0 No 45565 *Victoria*, was 24 minutes late away and further time was lost, resulting in a 40 minutes late departure for the combined train from Halifax, not a good start with only 16 miles completed and 346 to go.

Further delays occurred, so Hebden Bridge was passed 50 minutes late, and little had been gained by Chester. To everybody's delight, however, a magnificent red *Princess Royal* awaited us there for the journey to Llandudno Junction, and we also enjoyed several miles of parallel running with Class '5' No 45142 before the 'Pacific' pulled ahead - this was something that frequently happened on the North Wales route at summer weekends, with trains 'leap-frogging' one another to Llandudno.

Those of the party travelling clockwise round the circular trip to Blaenau Ffestiniog and Caernarvon were quickly away in their DMU, whilst *Princess Royal* was exchanged for two Stanier 2-6-2Ts, Nos 40116 and 40078, which gave a commendable performance anti-clockwise through Caernarvon to Portmadoc.

The passengers on the DMU had an eventful journey. About 3 miles past Bettws-y-Coed the leading axle of a bogie fractured, which distorted the bogie frame, resulting in 400 yards of damage to the track. Fortunately there happened to be a check rail at the spot which kept the bogie steady. Some branch committee members were soon on their way to find a

THE RAILWAY CORRESPONDENCE AND TRAVEL SOCIETY

ITINERARY OF THE
FESTINIOG SCENIC RAIL TOUR

LEEDS (CENTRAL)/BRADFORD (EXCHANGE) — HALIFAX — ROCHDALE MANCHESTER (EXCHANGE) — WARRINGTON (BANK QUAY) — CHESTER (GENERAL) — LLANDUDNO JCT. — CAERNARVON — AFON WEN PORTMADOC — FESTINIOG RLY. — TAN-Y-BWLCH — BLAENAU FFESTINIOG NORTH — BETTWS-Y-COED — LLANDUDNO JCT. — CHESTER (GENERAL) WARRINGTON (BANK QUAY)—MANCHESTER (EXCHANGE)—STALYBRIDGE HUDDERSFIELD — BRADFORD (EXCHANGE)/LEEDS (CITY)

SUNDAY, 22nd JULY, 1962

SCHEDULE

Mileage M. Ch.			Schedule a.m.
0.0	BRADFORD (EXCHANGE)	dep.	8-39
8.12	HALIFAX	arr.	8-53
0.0	LEEDS (CENTRAL)	dep.	8-40
7.65	LAISTERDYKE	pass	8-54
11.06	LOW MOOR	pass	9-00
16.22	HALIFAX	arr.	9-07
		dep.	9-13
24.74	HEBDEN BRIDGE	pass	9-25
29.32	TODMORDEN	pass	9-31
38.01	ROCHDALE	pass	9-42
48.62	MANCHESTER (EXCHANGE)	arr.	10-00
		dep.	10-02
65.21	EARLESTOWN	pass	10-26
70.22	WARRINGTON (BANK QUAY)	pass	10-35
88.25	CHESTER (GENERAL)	arr.	11-04
		dep.	11-16
118.18	RHYL	pass	11-54
			p.m.
132.49	LLANDUDNO JCT.	arr.	12-15
		dep.	12-25
156.39	CAERNARVON	arr.	1-00
		dep.	1-05
175.16	AFON WEN	arr.	1-48
		dep.	1-50
183.31	PORTMADOC	arr.	2-05

Mileage M. Ch.			Schedule p.m.
0.0	PORTMADOC	dep.	4-15
8.20	AFON WEN	arr.	4-30
		dep.	4-32
26.77	CAERNARVON	arr.	5-18
		dep.	5-25
50.67	LLANDUDNO JCT.	arr.	6-00
		dep.	6-10
65.18	RHYL	pass	6-30
95.11	CHESTER (GENERAL)	arr.	7-10
		dep.	7-22
113.14	WARRINGTON (BANK QUAY)	pass	7-55
118.15	EARLESTOWN	pass	8-02
134.54	MANCHESTER (EXCHANGE)	arr.	8-26
		dep.	8-28
142.69	STALYBRIDGE	pass	8-43
160.43	HUDDERSFIELD	arr.	9-11
		dep.	9-18
177.55	LEEDS CITY	arr.	9.49
	HUDDERSFIELD	dep.	9-24
165.72	BRIGHOUSE	pass	9-33
171.21	HALIFAX	arr.	9-45
		dep.	9-47
176.37	LOW MOOR	pass	9-54
179.33	BRADFORD (EXCHANGE)	arr.	10-00

Connecting Specials will run as follows :—

0.0	LLANDUDNO JCT.	dep.	12-30
15.01	BETTWS-Y-COED	pass	12-58
27.25	BLAENAU FFESTINIOG N.	arr.	1-25
	Thence by bus to		
0.0	TAN-Y-BWLCH	dep.	2-15
7.40	PORTMADOC (F. RLY.)	arr.	3-00

0.0	PORTMADOC (F. RLY.)	dep.	3-00
7.40	TAN-Y-BWLCH	arr.	3-45
	Thence by bus to		
0.0	BLAENAU FFESTINIOG N.	dep.	4-30
12.24	BETTWS-Y-COED	dep.	5-04
27.25	LLANDUDNO JCT.	arr.	5-32

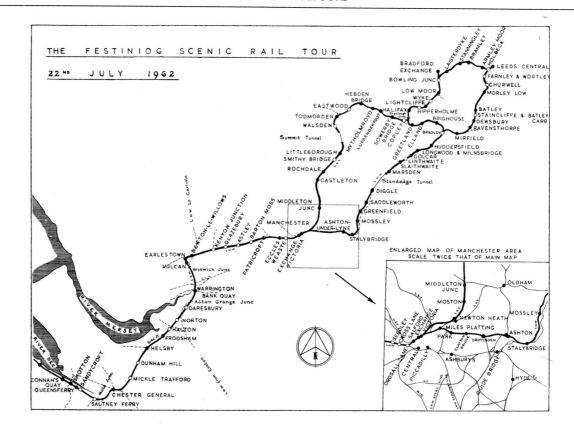

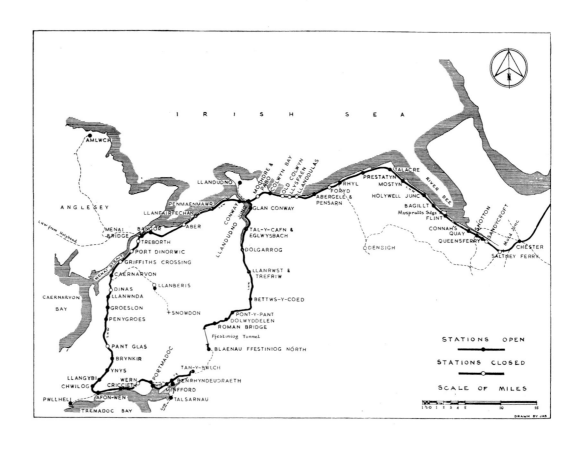

telephone in order to get the buses that were due to meet the tour at Blaenau Ffestiniog for the journey to Tan-y-Bwlch, to come to the rescue. They arrived with commendable speed and soon had the passengers on their way again, leaving the railwaymen to sort the problem.

The Festiniog Railway decided to combine the 3.35 pm service train with the RCTS special and the train left Tan-y-Bwlch with *Earl of Merioneth* at the head and *Prince* in the middle.

The buses then took the anti-clockwise party from Portmadoc to Bettws-y-Coed where a relief DMU was provided.

The resulting 68 minutes late departure from Llandudno Junction gave plenty incentive for the crew of *Princess Royal* to make up time, and with some brisk running 9 minutes were regained to Chester, where No 46145 was waiting to take over to Huddersfield.

Standard Class '5' No 73044 finished the journey for the Leeds passengers, while No 46145 then gave the best performance of the day to Halifax, gaining 13 minutes on the schedule for the 18 miles. The ascent of Greetland Bank to Salterhebble will long be remembered by those on the train.

So another West Riding tour was complete. Members Neil Fraser and F. Clough had compiled 14 foolscap pages of excellent notes regarding the history and the points of interest on the tour, for which the Society charged the princely sum of 1 shilling.

'Royal Scot' No 46145 *The Duke of Wellington's Regiment* waits patiently at Halifax for the arrival of the Leeds portion of the tour, before working through to Chester. This locomotive was allocated to Holbeck depot for many years for working the Scottish expresses over the Settle and Carlisle line. It was withdrawn four months after this tour and stored at Farnley Junction depot for about one year, before being steamed again for the last time to haul two other members of the class to Crewe Works for scrapping. *Gavin Morrison*

Left Caernarvon was, as can be seen in this picture, quite a spacious station. The Llandudno Junction Stanier 2-6-2Ts, Nos 40116 and 40078, working the anti-clockwise portion of the circular tour, paused for water. These locomotives were not one of the better Stanier designs in terms of performance, but on this occasion performed well. *Gavin Morrison*

Above Meanwhile, the RCTS headboard adorns the Festiniog Fairlie *Earl of Merioneth* as it finally arrives at Portmadoc with the clockwise party after all the troubles with the DMU near Bettws-y-Coed. *Gavin Morrison*

Right No 46200 *Princess Royal* at Llandudno Junction waiting to take the tour back to Chester. The red 'Pacific' was allocated to Carlisle Kingmoor at the time, and was primarily used on the trains to Perth. At the end of the year this locomotive, as well as other members of the class, was placed in store. *Gavin Morrison*

Sunday 7 October 1962
The Sussex Special Rail Tour

The tour was organised by the Sussex and Kent branch, and the participants arrived at London Bridge Station on a fine morning to see the most appropriate of locomotives, 'Schools' No 30925 *Cheltenham*, at the head of the train for what was probably the last opportunity to sample the capabilities of these magnificent locomotives on a fast main-line working.

The special had been timed at exactly 1 hour for the trip to Brighton, with seven coaches, which gave plenty of opportunity for the locomotive to show its paces. However, due to many unscheduled interruptions which it was estimated cost around 7 minutes, *Cheltenham* pulled into Brighton in 64 minutes after giving some magnificent hill-climbing and speeds in the mid-70s. Together with 17 other members of the class, *Cheltenham* was then only 10 weeks away from withdrawal, but happily the locomotive is now part of the National Railway Museum Collection.

A break of 1½ hours was taken at Brighton before the special continued, with appropriate motive power in the form of 'E-6' 0-6-2T No 32418, which was then 57 years old, piloted by the oldest locomotive in service with British Railways at that time, 0-6-0T 'Terrier' No 32636 (ex-LB&SCR *Fenchurch*), a month short of its 90th birthday. The special set off for Lewes and Seaford at 1.20 pm, with 50 mph being reached descending Falmer Bank.

'E4' 0-6-2T No 32479 was at Seaford to shunt the stock, before the train, the two locomotives running bunker first, headed for Newhaven, where they would be serviced and turned. Meanwhile a visit to the shed was made, and a real LB&SCR atmosphere prevailed as 'Terrier' No 32670 and 0-6-2T No 32503, together with the train locomotives, were all present.

The journey back to Brighton proved rather a struggle for the 'Terrier', but with the 'E6' it surmounted the 1 in 88 of Falmer Bank and got the train back to Brighton only 2¼ minutes late.

At Brighton the tanks were replaced by one of the handsome 'K' Class 2-6-0s built between 1913 and 1917. The tour locomotive, No 32353, had received a major overhaul at Eastleigh the previous in August, and was probably the last of the class to have one. The 'Mogul' gave a performance back to London

which was good enough to absorb some of the time lost by checks, so the arrival was just under a minute late.

So another tour came to an end, which must have delighted enthusiasts of Brighton-built locomotives as well as Southern steam in general.

Right Up until December 1972 'Schools' Class No 30925 *Cheltenham* appeared on the cover of the Society magazine, so it was appropriate that the locomotive should be used on some RCTS specials. Here the well turned out locomotive is seen ready to depart from London Bridge station on a 1-hour schedule to Brighton. It was built at Eastleigh in July 1934, and finally withdrawn for preservation in December 1962, just ten weeks after this tour. *Gavin Morrison*

THE RAILWAY CORRESPONDENCE AND TRAVEL SOCIETY

ITINERARY OF
THE SUSSEX SPECIAL RAIL TOUR

LONDON BRIGHTON & SOUTH COAST RAILWAY
1846

LONDON BRIDGE—BRIGHTON—SEAFORD
BRIGHTON—HORSHAM—SUTTON
PECKHAM RYE—LONDON BRIDGE

SUNDAY, 7th OCTOBER, 1962

The cover of the tour brochure, showing the RCTS 'Cheltenham' logo. *RCTS*

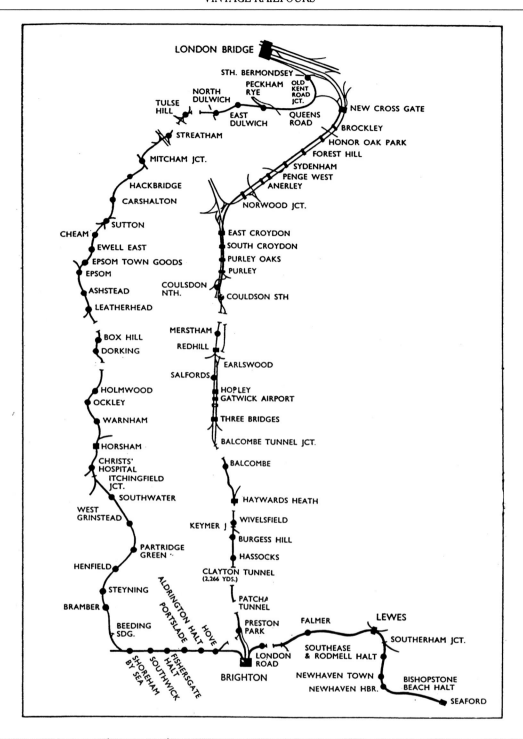

SCHEDULE

					Schedule						Schedule
					a.m.						p.m.
London Bridge ...	...	...	...	dep.	11-3	Newhaven Town	...	...	...	dep.	3-40
					p.m.	Brighton	...	...	...	arr.	4-17
Brighton	...	...	...	arr.	12-3					dep.	4-40
				dep.	1-20	Preston Park	...	...	...	arr.	4-44
Lewes ...	...	...	...	arr.	1-40					dep.	4-52
				dep.	1-53	Horsham ...	...	...	...	arr.	5-41
Seaford ...	...	...	...	arr.	2-14					dep.	5-46
				dep.	2-34	London Bridge ...	...	...	...	arr.	7-0
Newhaven Town	...	...	...	arr.	2-42						

'Terrier' No 32636, the former *Fenchurch,* was built in September 1872 and sold to Newhaven Harbour in 1898, where it remained until 1952. Here it pauses at Lewes coupled to the front of Billinton's 'E6' No 32418. The latter was withdrawn two months later after having covered 738,281 miles; the 'Terrier' is now preserved on the Bluebell Railway. *Gavin Morrison*

This was probably the last occasion on which a train arrived at Brighton headed by two ex-London, Brighton & South Coast locomotives, having returned with the special from Seaford. The train returned to London behind LB&SCR 'K' Class 'Mogul' No 32353. *Gavin Morrison*

Sundays 2 & 16 December 1962
The South Western Suburban Rail Tour

Bookings for this tour were so heavy that the joint committee of the RCTS and Stephenson Locomotive Society decided to run it on two weekends.

It was remarkable that after an absence from suburban duty of around 60 years, two of the famous Beattie 2-4-0Ts should return to run on suburban lines again. In terms of mileage, only 69^1/$_2$, the tour was short, but 56 miles were handled by the 1874-built Beyer-Peacock veterans. The weather was excellent on both weekends, and as can be seen from the photographs the locomotives were very well turned out.

The 210-ton six-coach train departed at 11.00 am from Waterloo for Hampton Court. The 550-gallon well tanks proved a problem for water capacity, and a severe overnight frost caused problems with the water supply at Hampton Court. However, prompt action by one of the Inspectors in obtaining the ser-

vices of the fire brigade avoided the need for one of the engines to drop its fire!

The train returned to Wimbledon, where 'H16' Class 4-6-2T No 30517 awaited the tour, again extremely well turned out, for the journey to Chessington South, a line never operated by suburban steam. On the return to Wimbledon the Beattie tanks were ready for the journey to Shepperton, whence the little engines ran bunker-first back to Waterloo.

The following week the tour ran smoothly, with the locos attached bunker-to-bunker. It was unbelievable that these two little tanks should finish their careers with a working into Waterloo. Happily they are both now preserved: No 30585 is at the Buckingham Railway Centre at Quainton Road, and No 30587 is part of the National Railway Museum Collection, at present on loan to the South Devon Railway for static display at Buckfastleigh.

Right The two Beattie veterans sparkle in the frosty morning sunshine at Surbiton before setting off the Hampton Court. Happily both locomotives are now preserved. *Gavin Morrison*

Below The special arrives at Hampton Court with the locomotives running bunker-first. *Gavin Morrison*

The Inspector and Guard keep a watchful eye as the locomotives are coupled up to the train before departing for Wimbledon. *Gavin Morrison*

Superbly turned out by Feltham depot for what must have been one of its very last duties, one of the five Urie 'H16' 4-6-2Ts, No 30517, is seen at Chessington during the tour. These locomotives spent most of their working careers on heavy freight around South London, with some empty carriage work at Clapham. *Gavin Morrison*

Saturday 4 May 1963
The Dalesman Rail Tour

1963 was an exceptionally busy year for the West Riding branch, as three main-line tours were run, the Dalesman being the first.

Bookings were very heavy, and the train was well over-subscribed. The attraction was, of course, the first outing of the preserved 'K4' No 3442 *The Great Marquess*, resplendent in LNER apple-green livery. The locomotive had been bought by Lord Garnock,

Embsay Junction is the setting for this picture of 'K4' No 3442 *The Great Marquess* as it prepares to be detached from the train to make a dash for Skipton to take water. The lines in the foreground are the Grassington branch, whilst the site of the Embsay Steam Railway preservation group now exists a few yards past the signal.

The locomotive entered service in July 1938 and remained at Eastfield depot for working the West Highland line until 1959, being then transferred to Thornton, from where it became the last of the class to be withdrawn in December 1961.

It worked south to Neville Hill depot at Leeds on 29 April 1963, where it was kept and used on specials, including one on Southern Region lines in 1967. In September 1972 it went to the Severn Valley Railway, where it can currently be seen working trains. *Gavin Morrison*

The Grassington branch was 10¹/₂ miles in length from Skipton and is still in use today to the Tilcon Quarry at Swinden, about 8 miles up the line. The branch lost its passenger service on 22 September 1930, and the section between Swinden limeworks and Grassington and Threshfield closed completely on 9 August 1969. In recent years the line has been visited by many specials, including an HST. The photograph shows the special in the yard at Grassington, together with many of the passengers. The station was demolished in 1978, and houses have been built on the site. *Gavin Morrison*

and before heading south it had visited Cowlairs works in Glasgow for painting and overhaul.

Departure from Bradford Forster Square was on time at 1.27 pm, for a scenic tour up the Yorkshire Dales and over to East Lancashire. The weather was good, and to help things along on the footplate Mr Albert Letham BEM was on board; he used to be a driver at Fort William and regularly drove the locomotive on the West Highland route. So everything seemed set for a trouble-free trip, but this was not to be.

It became apparent very early on - in fact on the steep bank out of Shipley to Guiseley - that the Gresley 'derived' valve gear was badly off, but in a series of surges the train made the summit successfully.

The trip up and down Wharfedale to turn on the triangle at Arthington went without incident, but at Embsay Junction the locomotive headed light engine for Skipton to take water and enable it to run round the train, which lost a lot of time.

The trip up the Grassington branch was followed by masses of cars on the road, and upon arrival it seemed that the entire village had turned out to see the train.

By the time Skipton was reached the tour was 40

minutes late and had lost its path down the line to Colne for a visit to the Barnoldswick branch, which at that time only had two trains per day for school children. A fifth run round was necessary at Earby before the train headed off for Blackburn, and an unscheduled stop for water at Colne put the special over an hour late.

The weather had also taken a turn for the worse, so photography came to an end. From Blackburn *The Great Marquess* headed for Hellifield. The crew didn't fancy tender-first running in the now heavy rain, so this resulted in another turning at Hellifield. Anxious passengers consulted timetables, and all came to the conclusion that it would be a very late arrival home - or may be not arriving at all.

Anyway, from Skipton the train had to go via Ilkley rather than the main line due to the locomotive being prohibited round the sharp curve at Shipley on to the Bradford line. Special stops were made *en route*, and a connection held at Shipley saw some passengers home, but the arrival at Forster Square 2½ hours late at 11.06 pm proved to be another record for the branch committee, one which they were not anxious to beat!

Little now remains of the site of Earby station on the Skipton-Colne line, opened in October 1848 and finally closed on 31 January 1970. *The Great Marquess* passes through the station heading for a trip along the Barnoldswick branch, which itself finally closed on 30 July 1966. *Gavin Morrison*

Sunday 30 June 1963
The Three Summits

The summits in question were Ais Gill, Beattock and Shap, although there were other minor summits as well, so with the motive power made up of two 'A4s', a 'Princess Coronation', the preserved Highland 'Jones Goods' and a Caledonian 0-6-0, we had the ingredients for a splendid day out. What we got as it turned out were the extremes of both disappointment and excitement, with brilliant performances from some of the crews, and terrible ones from others.

The report that appeared in the RCTS magazine, *the Railway Observer* No 415 of September 1963, from which I am obtaining most of my information about the tours, gave a rather scathing account of the day, which was perfectly accurate. However, this did not really appreciate the effort and skill that was put in on the trip north to Carlisle, to avoid what would have been a further major disappointment if 'A4' *Golden Eagle* had been removed from the train at Skipton due to injector failure. It was only the determination of one of Holbeck's top Scottish link drivers, Freddie Waites, that persuaded Inspector Albert Pullan that they should carry on with the 'A4' after emergency repairs at Skipton, alongside the shed.

On this occasion I can speak with first-hand knowledge as I was privileged to be travelling on the footplate. As it turned out further trouble occurred with the injector by about Bell Busk. It was no mean feat for the crew to get us to Blea Moor as well as they did, and by then the water in the glass had virtually disappeared, and it was not until we were descending Mallerstang Common that *Golden Eagle* could be opened up.

What then followed was a time from Ais Gill to Carlisle of 41 min 55 sec for the 48¼ miles, giving an average of 78.4 mph, including a restriction of 70 mph near Armathwaite, and speeds up to 90 mph. I can confirm that the driver would have gone even faster and probably reached 100 mph around Ormside, had not the Inspector decided otherwise. The riding of the locomotive was superb, which was not only a credit to the 'A4' but also to the state of the track in those days.

So the 76.8 miles from Hellifield to Carlisle had been reeled off in 82½ minutes, with a 360-ton train

TABLE II			
SETTLE & CARLISLE LINE: DOWNHILL SPEED MALLERSTANG-CUMWHINTON			
Year		1902	1963
Engine No.		2607	60023
„ Class		M.R. 4-4-0	L.N.E.R. "A4"
Load, tons full		320	360
Dist.		Actual	Actual
Miles		m. s.	m. s.
0.0	Mallerstang Box ...	0 00*	0 00*
3.3	Kirkby Stephen ...	2 39	3 04
6.5	Crosby Garrett ...	5 01	5 47
11.6	Ormside ...	8 37	9 17
14.0	APPLEBY ...	10 24	10 57
16.9	Long Marton ...	12 34	13 04
21.4	Culgaith ...	15 58	16 15
25.1	Langwathby ...	18 45	18 47
26.5	Little Salkeld ...	19 50	19 46
29.6	LAZONBY ...	22 04	21 56
34.8	Armathwaite ...	26 55	26 25
40.9	Cumwhinton ...	32 12	31 17
Average speeds, m.p.h. ...		76.3 ·	78.4

* Times from passing Mallerstang at full speed.

Courtesy of The Railway Magazine

and a partly failed engine. It was of interest to note that another 'A4', No 60002 *Sir Murray Wilson*, was passed heading south near Baron Wood, so the Settle and Carlisle line had two 'A4s' in one day working over it, which was virtually unheard of, except possible during the diversions as a result of the floods in the Scottish Borders during 1948.

Golden Eagle left the train at Carlisle with a promise from the crew that all would be sorted out with the injector before we returned. It was replaced by 'Princess Coronation' No 46255 *City of Hereford*, and the tour departed 50 minutes late, which was plenty of incentive for some fine running.

We were not disappointed. After a cautious departure from the Carlisle area, the 'Coronation' really got into her stride, and had gained no less than 10 minutes by Beattock. The bank was being climbed in fine style until detonators announced that work was being done on a timber bridge at milepost 44, and this brought the speed down to 10 mph.

The 360-ton train was worked back up to 35 mph by the summit, with some splendid music from the exhaust. In spite of the delay we were 15 minutes up on schedule by the summit, but more wrong line working resulted in an overall ½ minute gain to

Carstairs. This was a fine performance from the crew, who it was said were unfamiliar with working 'Pacifics' and fast passenger trains.

At Carstairs the preserved 'Jones Goods' with Caledonian 0-6-0 No 57581 backed on to give us a pleasant amble across the countryside to Auckinleck.

Here 'A4' No 60004 *William Whitelaw* was waiting, but the less said about the journey to Carlisle the better - it was probably the most uninspired run behind an 'A4' I had ever experienced, so we were still 33 minutes down on arrival. The photographers had to be quick to get a picture of the two 'A4s' side up side as *William Whitelaw* was exchanged for *Golden Eagle*. We were informed that the injector problems had been solved, and a good climb to Shap was promised.

This hope was, however, dashed before we even started, as Control decided to let the 7.15 pm DMU to Keswick out directly in front of us. The tour thus departed 47 minutes late, but the 'A4' was soon producing some superb climbing. By Plumpton we were travelling at 66 mph and still accelerating, already having gained 5 minutes on the schedule, but we all knew we would eventually be checked by the DMU, and so

it proved, for we were stopped for 3 minutes outside Penrith, which must have cost us at least 9 minutes.

In spite of this major disappointment, driver Freddie Waites and fireman Peter Chambers did their best, to such an extent that the train was worked up to 60 mph by Shap Summit box, which was a terrific achievement. We can only speculate what might have been, but we would probably have averaged very nearly 60 mph from Carlisle to the summit.

We shot down the bank passing Scout Green at 82 mph before applying the brakes for a stop at Tebay to drop off a pilotman. Opportunities for fast running were now over, but the locomotive was worked very hard where possible over the Ingleton line to Clapham Junction. It was very interesting to note that we had achieved a net time of around 89 minutes to Hellifield from Carlisle, faster than the normal non-stop schedule at that time over the Settle and Carlisle line.

This was another very fine tour, and as was common with the West Riding events - the unexpected had happened, resulting in disappointment, but also giving rise to some superb locomotive performances due to the delays.

It is usually the crew who are really responsible for making a tour a success or not - they do the hard work but seldom get their pictures taken. I am glad therefore to be able to include this famous trio from Holbeck depot. In the centre is Inspector Albert Pullan who accompanied us on many of our tours until his retirement, when Inspector Geoff Wilson took over. On his right, on the platform, is Driver Freddie Waites, one of the senior men in the Glasgow link at the time, with his fireman Peter Chambers on the footplate. The picture was taken at Leeds City prior to departure with 'A4' No 60023 *Golden Eagle*.
Gavin Morrison

As discussions on the footplate were taking place regarding the faulty injector, there was time to take this picture of *Golden Eagle* at Skipton. Built in December 1936, it survived until October 1964, having spent the majority of its working career allocated to Gateshead, from January 1942 to October 1963, when it went to St Margaret's, before moving to Aberdeen Ferryhill five months before its withdrawal. *Gavin Morrison*

The 'Princess Coronation' *City of Hereford* was soon removed from the train at Carstairs and Caledonian 0-6-0 No 57581 and the famous Highland 'Jones Goods' 4-6-0 No 103 backed on. The latter locomotive was built in September 1894 by Sharp Stewart and lasted until October 1934, its LMS number being 17916, and the distinctive louvred chimney came in fact from locomotive No 17919. After repainting, the locomotive went to Inverness for exhibition in 1935, but then returned to St Rollox Works out of public view, being left outside during the war, causing some deterioration. In 1946 it was taken back inside and repainted, but nothing happened until 1958 when the General Manager of the Scottish Region, James Ness, decided it should be returned to working order, and it then travelled extensively around the Region until 6 July 1966 when it was retired and moved to the Glasgow Museum of Transport. *Gavin Morrison*

The 'Jones Goods' and Caledonian 0-6-0 No 57581 make a spirited departure from Muirkirk on the now long-closed line from Carstairs to Auchinleck. The line to Muirkirk from Carstairs was originally Caledonian, becoming Glasgow & South Western onwards to Auchinleck. *Rodney Lissenden*

There was time to photograph the two veterans before they left the train at Auchinleck. No 57581 was one of the McIntosh '812' Class built between 1899 and 1909. The last of the class was withdrawn in 1963. *Gavin Morrison*

'A4' No 60004 *William Whitelaw* took over the tour at Auchinleck for the run to Carlisle. The locomotive was built in November 1937; originally named *Great Snipe*, it was renamed in July 1941. It spent most of its working days as part of Haymarket's allocation, joining in July 1941 and spending 21 years at the depot before moving to Aberdeen Ferryhill, from where it was withdrawn in July 1966. The 'A4' is seen here at the head of the special near New Cumnock, making its leisurely way to Carlisle. This particular locomotive was used on three separate RCTS tours. *Rodney Lissenden*

Saturday 19 October 1963
The Nidd Valley Special

This tour must surely have been the most leisurely ever organised by the West Riding branch - just over seven hours were allowed for the 85 miles, with seven stops for photographs. It was the last train to Pateley Bridge, which had in fact lost is passenger service 12 years previously.

The 230 passengers gathered on platform 11 at Leeds to join the six-coach special, headed by commendably clean Fowler 2-6-4T No 42409 from Holbeck depot.

The outward journey was to Wetherby via Church Fenton and Tadcaster, a line which in 1963 was served by one passenger train per day in one direction only!

Whilst running round at Wetherby a Newcastle-Liverpool express passed headed by an English Electric diesel-electric, later Class '40'. No 42409 then set off 1 minute early and tackled the steep gradients to Harrogate in fine style, crossing the famous Crimple Viaduct on the outskirts of the town.

At Harrogate the Chairman of the Pateley Bridge and Ripon Rural District Council, together with the Clerk to the Council, joined the special for a last run

along the branch. Also on board was the driver of the last excursion to have been run over the branch, headed by a 'D49' in 1949.

We joined the branch at Ripley Junction, and had plenty of time to look at the countryside as the official speed limit was 10 mph. The local population turned out in force at all the intermediate stations - Hampsthwaite, Birstwith, Darley and Dacre - and 5 minutes late departure from Harrogate was turned into a 38 minutes early arrival at Pateley Bridge.

The station had probably never seen so many people - half the local population appeared to have turned out. Plenty of time was allowed for the passengers to explore the remains of the Nidd Valley Light Railway, visit the local pubs which happened to be open, or wander around the town. The press arrived to interview and photograph the train crew, so a jolly time was had by all on what was in fact a very sad day, as yet another rural town lost its connection to the main railway network.

The return journey to Leeds was uneventful, and in contrast to tours run earlier in the year our arrival back was 24 minutes early.

Mls.	Chs.	SCHEDULE		Schedule p.m.	Actual p.m.
-	-	Leeds (City) South	Depart	12.40	
9	56	Micklefield	Pass	12/55	
14	65	Church Fenton	Pass	1/ 2	
26	13	Wetherby	Arrive	1.27	
		"	Depart	1.42	
34	03	Harrogate	Arrive	1.57	
		"	Depart	2. 4	
37	00	Ripley Junction	Pass	2/12	
40	58	Birstwith	Arrive	2.36	
		"	Depart	2.46	
43	34	Darley	Arrive	3.14	
			Depart	3.24	
44	75	Dacre	Arrive	3.36	
		"	Depart	3.46	
48	39	Pateley Bridge	Arrive	4.22	
		" "	Depart	5.12	
59	78	Ripley Junction	Pass	6/47	
62	75	Harrogate	Arrive	6.54	
		"	Depart	7. 2	
70	65	Wetherby	Pass	7/16	
81	03	Cross Gates	Pass	7/37	
85	36	Leeds (City) South	Arrive	7.47	

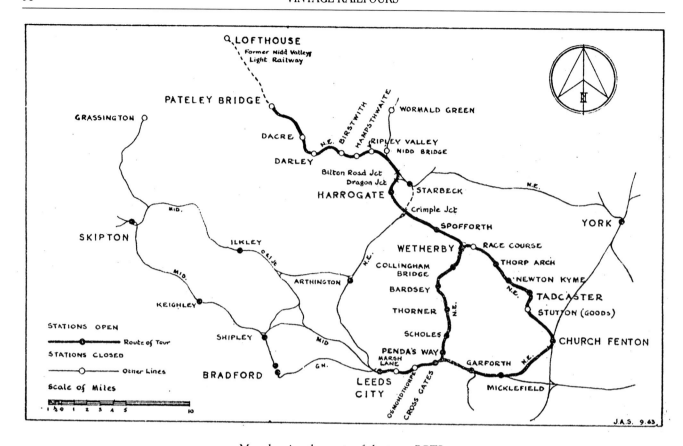

Map showing the route of the tour. *RCTS*

Gradient profile of the branch from Ripley Junction to Pateley Bridge, drawn for the tour brochure. *RCTS*

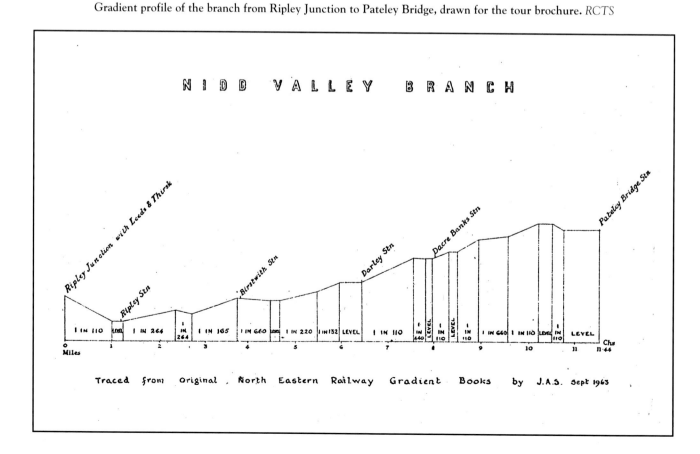

The special approaches Harrogate on the outward journey with Fowler 2-6-4T No 42409 running bunker-first. *Howard Malham*

The state of the track at Pateley Bridge indicates that closure is imminent, and as the train prepares to leave the light rapidly fails. No 42409 was withdrawn in 1964; the last two examples of the class, Nos 42394 and 42410, finished their working days in the Leeds/Bradford area in 1966. *Gavin Morrison*

Holbeck depot always made an effort to clean the locomotive for the RCTS West Riding branch tours when one of theirs was diagrammed. Looking immaculate inside the gloom of the roundhouse, Fowler 2-6-4T No 42409 waits to be lit up before working the Nidd Valley special the following day. *Gavin Morrison*

Sunday 22 March 1964
The Sussex Downsman

This was a joint tour between the RCTS and the Locomotive Club of Great Britain, and was to be one of the last, if not the very last, steam-operated tours over the London, Brighton & South Coast system.

Waterloo station was the starting point and 'Q1' 0-6-0 No 33027 departed with a well-filled 302-ton train. After a slow for a landslip near Effingham, the versatile 'Q1' was worked up to 64 mph through West Clandon. The train then took the single line to Horsham at Peasmarsh Junction, and a photo-stop was made at Cranleigh.

Horsham was left on time behind immaculate 'N' Class 2-6-0 No 31411, and a maximum of 64 mph was achieved on the main line as the special worked round to Three Bridges, where No 33027 re-joined the train again after travelling direct from Horsham. The special then travelled via East Grinstead to Tunbridge Wells, where the 'Q1' was exchanged for superb 'Battle of Britain' 'Pacific' No 34066 *Spitfire*, well known for its involvement in the 1957 Lewisham rail disaster.

The tour then followed the 'Cuckoo line' through the beautiful Wealdon countryside. At Pevensey 'N' Class No 31411 took over again, and the train visited the old station at Lewes before proceeding to Brighton.

At Brighton the party transferred to a seven-coach train headed by Ivatt Class '2' 2-6-2T No 41287 for the short run to Kemp Town. *Spitfire* then ran up from Pevensey to head the special back to Victoria via Uckfield, reaching 73 mph at Edenbridge.

Arrival back in London was a few minutes late, but this did not detract from a memorable day out with steam around the ex-London, Brighton & South Coast lines.

One of the very handsome 'N' Class 'Moguls', No 31411, in very fine condition, worked the special from Horsham to Three Bridges via Shoreham, and is seen here heading the train near Partridge Green. The locomotive entered traffic in November 1930, and was first allocated to Bricklayers Arms. It was one of the six locomotives of the class to receive a general overhaul at Eastleigh in May 1963, before being finally withdrawn in April 1966. *Hugh Ballantyne*

Left The changeover of motive power at Tunbridge Wells West is illustrated in this picture. Un-rebuilt 'Battle of Britain' 'Pacific' No 34066 *Spitfire* waits for the guard's green flag. Built in September 1947, it entered traffic as No 21C166, being re-numbered in February 1949 and covering 652,908 miles until withdrawal in September 1966. *Spitfire* was originally allocated to Ramsgate depot, and was eventually broken up by J. Battigieg of Newport, Monmouth. The main event in the locomotive's career was its involvement in the disastrous St Johns, Lewisham, accident on 4 December 1957, when it was the locomotive working the delayed 4.56 pm Cannon Street-Dover which ran into the back of the 5.18 pm Charing Cross-Hayes electric train. The locomotive was not badly damaged and returned to traffic on 22 March 1958. 'Q1' No 33027 stands on the right, having worked from Three Bridges. *Hugh Ballantyne*

Above Working in from Three Bridges, 'Q1' No 33027 passes the signal box at East Grinstead; the signalman is about to collect the token. This locomotive built as No C27 in July 1942, and was a member of the last batch to survive, until January 1966. It was built at Ashford Works, and while the design may not have been everybody's idea of a beautiful locomotive, they were certainly good performers. The highest mileage achieved by any member of the class was 500,663 miles. No 33027 was used for several special workings in 1964 and 1965 and, together with No 33020, it was used on the last steam workings on the Central Section on 3 October 1965. Fortunately No C1, or No 33001, is now preserved in working order on the Bluebell Railway. *Hugh Ballantyne*

Saturday 25 April 1964
North Yorkshireman Rail Tour

It was a dull and dismal morning as the passengers for the tour gathered at Leeds to board the nine-coach special, not the best of weather conditions for a tour of the Dales. Leeds City station was still in some disarray as a result of a mishap the previous evening when a Class '25' on the 'Devonian' had collided with a DMU. In spite of this, departure was only 8 minutes late.

This was another tour of 'lasts', as it was to be the last train on the Redmire branch through to Hawes, and what was believed to be the last passenger work-ing of one of the few remaining 'B16/2' 4-6-0s, No 61435, which had been well groomed for the occasion. No 61435 was to be the last of the class to be withdrawn, three months after this tour. What a pity one of these fine machines was not preserved.

In spite of a good climb up to Bramhope Tunnel, time was dropped to Harrogate, where the first engine change took place. Rather unexpectedly York had provided a very dirty Carlisle Kingmoor Class '5', No 44790, for the trip down the Boroughbridge branch.

Very dirty Kingmoor Class '5' No 44790 passes Copgrove station on the outward journey to Boroughbridge; Class '5s' were very rare visitors to the line. No 44790 was withdrawn in 1967 from Kingmoor depot, along with 305 other members of the class that year. *Gavin Morrison*

After running round at the terminus, the return journey was made tender first to Starbeck where the 'B16/2' took over again.

Once more the locomotive started to gain time until an absent crossing-keeper caused a delay which made the arrival at Northallerton 24 minutes late. Water was taken, and some time regained, until immediately after departure it was discovered that one of the committee members appeared to have been left behind. The train was halted, but he was found further up the train.

As we headed through the beautiful countryside of Wensleydale the day began to brighten, but knowing that there was complicated shunting to be done at Hawes, involving the splitting of the train, it was decided to pass Aysgarth non-stop. Regrettably this was an omission from the advertised programme, but it did regain a lot of time.

As always the locals turned out in force to wave their farewells to the line, although this had not been the case when the service from Hawes to Garsdale had been withdrawn on 16 March 1959, the through passenger service to Northallerton having been withdrawn in April 1954.

The schedule for the whole tour was rather optimistic, and in spite of good running back along the valley the train was 30 minutes late at Wensley. After watering at Leyburn the 'B16/2' made a rapid run to Castle Hill Junction in spite of the tender-first running in the rain.

Here to take over the tour was the unusual combination of Gresley 'V3' 2-6-2T No 67646 coupled bunker-to-bunker with Stanier 2-6-4T No 42639, which had been done for the benefit of the photographers, but somehow didn't seem to look quite right.

The committee members were getting anxious about the lateness as an optional coach tour had been organised from Middleton-in-Teesdale to High Force, and it was realised that we were unlikely to get in front of the 16.35 DMU from Darlington to Middleton. Our worst fears were confirmed when, in spite of setting off briskly down the main line, the special was put on to the slow line at Cowton to let the down 'Queen of Scots' and the 10.40 Bristol-Newcastle past, so by the time we passed Darlington we were an hour late. It was obvious that the coach trip would have to be abandoned, so the committee had to refund 132 bookings. By the time Middleton was reached the lateness had increased to 75 minutes. The planned lengthy stay was reduced to half an hour, which got the arrears down to 17 minutes.

The final loco change of the day took place at Darlington, where 'V2' No 60855 was waiting. The hoped-for dash up the main line to York started well with speed around the 80 mph mark near Thirsk, until permanent way workings ruined the run near Pilmoor.

Again the crew did their best from York, and made a splendid ascent of Micklefield Bank, so the arrival was only 19 minutes down, something which the committee could not have hoped for as the train headed towards Middleton-in-Teesdale!

There was little sign of activity at Boroughbridge as the special arrived, although some of the locals had put up some bunting on the station to welcome the train. Passenger services had been withdrawn in September 1950, when the line continued through to Pilmoor on the East Coast Main Line, the service having been primarily worked by Starbeck depot 'G5s'. *Gavin Morrison*

'B16/2' No 61435 makes a fine sight as it heads up Wensleydale through Leyburn station. It was 10 years earlier, almost to the day, that the section of line between Hawes and Garsdale saw its last passenger train, and almost 30 years later, on 2 January 1993, the line as far as Redmire closed completely. Leyburn station still stands, although the line was singled and the platform on the left removed. It was a popular branch for rail tours in recent years, including even an HST. The last daily workings to the quarry at Redmire were worked by Class '60' locomotives, the last freight train running on 18 December 1992. *Gavin Morrison*

No 61435 in the middle of the complicated manoeuvres at Hawes necessary to
enable it to run round the train. The line
north to Garsdale to join the Settle and
Carlisle line closed on 14 March 1959.
Two days after the passage of the special
from Hawes back to Redmire, the section of line was officially closed to all
traffic. The 'B16/2' was the last of the
class to be withdrawn three months after
the tour. What a pity this fine locomotive slipped through the preservation net.
Gavin Morrison

Now running extremely late, the special
pauses at Barnard Castle on its way to
Middleton-in-Teesdale. 'V3' No 67646
was still showing a Heaton shedplate,
although it was actually allocated to
Gateshead, having been transferred when
Heaton closed on 16 June 1963. The
locomotive survived until November
1964, being a member of the last batch to
be withdrawn. Stanier 2-6-4T No 42639
was at Darlington and was also withdrawn later in the year. *Gavin Morrison*

The tour is seen drifting into Middleton-in-Teesdale over the viaduct, 75 minutes late. The regular trains were operated by DMUs, but not long after this tour, on 30 November 1964, the service was to be withdrawn, with all traffic finishing on 5 April the following year. *Gavin Morrison*

Sunday 3 May 1964   The Cornubian

This was a joint tour between the RCTS and the Plymouth Railway Circle, and was organised to mark the end of steam over the main line through Cornwall to Penzance.

Suitable steam locomotives, or any steam locos for that matter, in this part of the country were getting rare - the choice of Churchward 2-8-0 No 2887 to

work between Exeter and Plymouth, with 'West Country' 'Pacific' No 34002 *Salisbury* onwards to Penzance reflected this situation.

No 2887 with a Taunton crew was at the head of the train ready to depart from Exeter St Davids on a bright sunny morning. The journey to Plymouth involved the locomotive having to reverse the train back over the summit at Dainton, then up the 1 in 36 from a standing start back through the tunnel for wrong line working to Totnes, which resulted in arrival 10 minutes late.

Smartly turned out 'West Country' No 34002 *Salisbury* backed on to the train and was soon on its way to the first booked stop at Bodmin Road, where the first of the civic receptions took place, followed by another at Truro. A pause was made at Redruth, where the Rural District Officers were waiting. At this point there were over 300 on board, and Penzance was reached a few minutes early to be greeted by vast crowds as well as the Lady Mayor and other dignitaries.

After an hour the return journey commenced, with *Salisbury* performing well. All credit was due to the crew, who had never worked a 'West Country' before, and spoke well of the locomotive, but it was a pity that a GWR locomotive could not have been made available to mark the end of steam on the main line in Cornwall.

No 2887 took over again at Plymouth, and made excellent climbs of Hemerdon and Dainton, just as these locomotives used to do in years gone by with Summer Saturday extras. Exeter was reached early, and so ended another successful tour, even if the occasion must have been a sad one for many steam enthusiasts.

The shortage of suitable ex-Great Western locomotives in the Somerset/Devon/Cornwall area by May 1964 resulted in a rather dirty Churchward 2-8-0, No 2887, being chosen to head the special to Plymouth. Constructed in March 1938 it was one of the 83 built between that year and 1942, virtually to an identical specification to the previous 84 locomotives, the last of which, No 2883, had been completed in April 1919, such was the excellence of the design. These locomotives were used frequently on Summer Saturdays, hauling extra trains over the steep inclines, so from that point of view at least the locomotive was a suitable choice. It is seen here ready to leave Exeter St Davids. *Hugh Ballantyne*

Above 'Bodmin Road, change for Bodmin, Wadebridge and Padstow' says the sign to the left of the locomotive. The Mayor with his gold chain of office can be seen heading towards the locomotive, un-rebuilt Bulleid 'light Pacific' No 34002 *Salisbury*, which was in fine external condition. Built in June 1945, it was to survive until April 1967, and was one of the two members of the class to cover more than 1 million miles in service. The other with the highest total was No 34006 with 1,099,338. These locomotives were rarely seen on the GWR main line to Penzance, but the Western Region crew were very impressed with *Salisbury*'s performance, in spite of it being the first time they had been on a 'West Country'. *Hugh Ballantyne*

Left and right There was not much free space at Penzance, either on the tracks or on the platform, as the passengers and local people turned out in force to witness the historic event. *Hugh Ballantyne*

The special pauses at Redruth on the return journey from Penzance to Plymouth. *Hugh Ballantyne*

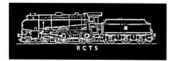

9 May 1964   East Midlander No 7

Appropriately, 'Princess Coronation' No 46251 *City of Nottingham* was the locomotive selected to head this tour out of its 'home' city to Swindon and Eastleigh. It was in fact its second visit, having attended a naming ceremony here in 1946.

At 7.35 am the tour departed with 500 passengers on board, heading up the old Great Central main line to Woodford Halse, and then across to Banbury, Oxford and Didcot, where the locomotive was replaced by 'West Country' 'light Pacific' No 34038 *Lynton* for the journey to Eastleigh.

At Eastleigh the 'Pacific' was replaced by 'USA' 0-6-0T No 30071 to haul the 400-ton train into the Works. Some doubted its ability to do so, but it carried out the task without difficulty.

Lynton then performed well to Swindon, where *City of Nottingham*, having run light from Didcot, had been placed alongside No 7022 *Hereford Castle* at the shed, to give the unusual sight of an LMS 'Pacific' alongside a GWR 'Castle'.

The return journey went well back to Didcot, where arrival was 1¹/₂ minutes early, but then followed a series of checks all the way to Banbury, where the special rejoined the Great Central line nearly 15 minutes late. Many restrictions on the route back to Nottingham prevented the big 'Pacific' from really showing its capabilities, although there were a few bursts of real power accelerating away from slacks.

Spotless 'Princess Coronation' No 46251 *City of Nottingham* passes Appleford *en route* to Didcot. *Rodney Lissenden*

Having taken over from the LMS 'Pacific' at Didcot, un-rebuilt Bulleid 'light Pacific' No 34038 *Lynton* is seen heading south from Didcot on the ex-Didcot, Newbury & Southampton line through to Winchester. No 34038 entered service in September 1946 and lasted until June 1966, having covered 819,984 miles in service. *Rodney Lissenden*

Further along the DN&S line *Lynton* is shown passing the ugly signal box at Highclere, heading for Eastleigh. *Hugh Ballantyne*

A fine study of *City of Nottingham* taken in the yard of Swindon Works, before setting off towards Didcot and back to Nottingham. Built at Crewe in June 1944 as a streamlined locomotive at a cost of £11,664, it was allocated to all the main West Coast Main Line depots, finishing up at Crewe. At the time of this tour the locomotive had only four months left before withdrawal, and was in first class condition, as were many of these fine locomotives at the end of their lives. No 46251 was withdrawn on 12 September, having averaged over 63,000 miles per annum during its working days. *Hugh Ballantyne*

City of Nottingham stands amongst ex-GWR locomotives on Swindon Shed. There must have been many ex-Great Western employees at Swindon who would never have believed that a Stanier 'Pacific' would visit the depot and be photographed alongside one of their 'Castles'! It would be inappropriate of me in this book to draw comparisons between the locomotives shown, but even the most diehard GWR enthusiasts must have admitted that *City of Nottingham* made a very fine sight in its red livery.
Hugh Ballantyne

Saturday 23 May 1964
The Ribble-Lune Rail Tour

The Lancashire and North West branch organised this tour around Lancashire, with a brief excursion into Yorkshire. The motive power was of interest in that I believe it was the only occasion on which a British Railways Standard 'Clan' 'Pacific' was rostered to haul an RCTS tour.

No 72007 *Clan Mackintosh* of Kingmoor was turned out looking very smart, with a five-coach train plus a Buffet car. Some would say that it was about the right load for one of these engines, which never seemed to receive much praise from the crews, possibly because when new they were diagrammed for the heavy Manchester/Liverpool-Glasgow expresses, which were possibly beyond their capabilities. Never the less, many considered them to be the most handsome of the Standard designs.

The special departed from Preston at 13.15, but neither the schedule nor the route gave any possibility of producing anything of note for the stopwatch brigade. The West Lancashire route to Southport was followed, then the spur to Meols Cop was taken for Burscough. The North Curve to Burscough North Junction was followed by the Liverpool-Preston line, then the unusual route via Lostock Hall and the spur to the Blackburn line. Thence the itinerary took the train to Hellifield with a photographic stop at Gisburn.

Water was taken at Hellifield, then the special proceeded via Wennington Junction to Lancaster Green Ayre, travelling to Morecambe on the electrified line. The curve at Torrisholme provided some rare track *en route* to Heysham Harbour, the train being hauled back to Morecambe by Ivatt 2-6-0 No 46441 while the 'Clan' turned.

The return to Green Ayre was made with the 'Clan' running tender first; it ran round then went up to Lancaster Castle, before reversing from Lancaster No 1 box down to Lancaster (old) station.

Here the passengers had plenty of time to photograph the train and wander around before the tour returned to the main line and on to Preston. The hoped for a dash down the main line unfortunately did not materialise due to a preceding train, and the tour terminated a few minutes early.

Left Displaying the fine proportions of the class, No 72007 *Clan Mackintosh* simmers in the sun at Lancaster old goods yard while the passengers take their pictures, before heading back up the main line to Preston. The locomotive was allocated to Carlisle Kingmoor for its entire working life, from February 1952 to December 1965. *Gavin Morrison*

Right *Clan Mackintosh* makes a fine sight as it takes water at Hellifield, before heading off for Morecambe. *Gavin Morrison*

Having returned from Morecambe 'under the wires' tender first, the 'Clan' ran round the train at Lancaster Green Ayre before setting off up the spur to the West Coast Main Line. In the background can be seen a Stanier '8F' simmering in the yard of the locomotive depot. *Gavin Morrison*

Saturday 13 June 1964
The Solway Ranger

The West Riding branch organised many splendid and ambitious tours over the years, but this was probably the finest. Authority had been given for a 'Merchant Navy' from Nine Elms, together with a crew from that depot, to work the special over Shap and the Settle and Carlisle line. This was probably the first time that a 'Merchant Navy' had been in Leeds since the 1948 trails, and certainly the first for a rebuilt example of the class.

The locomotive, which turned out to be No 35012 *United States Lines*, duly arrived at Holbeck depot on the Friday evening together with RCTS member Bert Hooker as the driver and fireman Seaby. Interestingly, Bert Hooker had been the fireman during the Locomotive Exchanges when 'West Country' No 34004 *Yeovil* was used over Shap.

THE
RAILWAY CORRESPONDENCE AND
TRAVEL SOCIETY

M.N. PACIFIC

MAP and ITINERARY
1X37
SOLWAY RANGER RAIL TOUR

LEEDS — SKIPTON — CARNFORTH — SHAP — PENRITH — WORKINGTON
ROWRAH — SELLAFIELD — WHITEHAVEN — MARYPORT — CARLISLE
SILLOTH — CARLISLE — AIS GILL — SKIPTON — LEEDS

SATURDAY, 13th JUNE, 1964

So, with 365 miles of steam traction, and motive power provided by the 'Merchant Navy', two Ivatt 2-6-0s, the preserved Scottish Caledonian 'Single' No 123, and Great North of Scotland 4-4-0 *Gordon Highlander*, plus 80 miles with a DMU, it would have been hard to come up with a better variety.

It was a dull morning as *United States Lines* made a punctual start at 8.43 am, which immediately resulted in two signal checks before the platform was clear! But the schedule to Carnforth was very easy; on arrival, the train was pulled from the Midland line on to the West Coast route by Stanier Class '5 'No 45394, a local engine.

The placid running so far was about to change, as Bert Hooker was obviously determined to show the passengers, and no doubt the LM Authorities, just what a 'Merchant Navy' could do over the line. Everything was set just right, as we were 7 minutes late.

With a moderate load of nine coaches, we were treated to a run the likes of which few had experienced over Grayrigg and up Shap. The climb out of Carnforth at 1 in 134 was attacked with vigour, followed by the slight downhill stretch before Milnthorpe, where we were doing 68 mph, the $7^1/_2$ miles from the start being covered in 10 min 12 sec. After a further 6 miles of climbing we were through Oxenholme at 60 mph in 15 min 25 sec, and we were still travelling at 54.5 mph at milepost 22. Speed then increased to 60 mph up the 1 in 131/106 to Grayrigg, which was passed in 22 min 55 sec, 20 miles from a standing start to Grayrigg Summit having been covered in just under 23 minutes.

By Dillicar we were doing an outstanding 82.5 mph, and started the climb to Shap at 77.5 mph, 27 min 54 sec from Carnforth. Speed had only dropped to 75 mph as we approached Scout Green, passed in 30 min 26 sec, but it was not to last, for Control, as on another epic climb to Shap but that time heading south with 'A4' No 60023, had managed to let a train out in front, and we came to a dead stand at Shap Wells.

It is certain that we could have passed the summit doing at least 60 mph, so once again the passengers were robbed of a clear run. It must have been a terrible disappointment to Bert Hooker, and no doubt to fireman Seabey who must have worked very hard indeed. So we eventually reached Penrith in 1 second under the hour from Carnforth, 7 minutes over the schedule.

The two Upperby-allocated Ivatt 2-6-0s, No 46426 and 46458, took over to Workington, giving a spirited climb up the bank to Troutbeck Summit. At Workington passengers transferred to a six-coach Derby-built DMU for the trip to Moor Row and Rowrah, then through to Sellafield and back to Carlisle.

The weather by now was sunny and the Scottish preserved locomotives made a very colourful sight as

they backed on to the special for the journey over the tightly curved line to Silloth, which by contrast presented a depressing picture as closure was not far away. The locomotives turned on the turntable and, to much whistling, set off back. It seemed that the whole town had turned out to see the train.

At the RCTS meeting on the Friday night Bert Hooker had promised he would give us a ride to remember over the Settle and Carlisle line, and he certainly didn't disappoint us.

I was very lucky to be travelling on the footplate, together with a Holbeck driver from the Scottish link as conductor. Again the incentive was there to

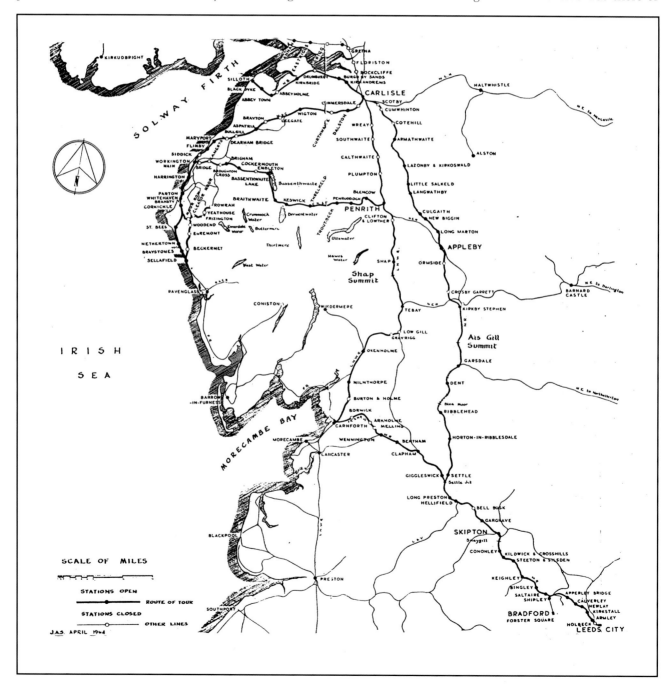

1X37 TIMINGS

M. Ch.	Station		a.m.
0 00	Leeds City South	D	8-43
10 57	Shipley/Leeds Junc.		9-0
17 00	Keighley		9-12
25 01	Snaygill		9-27
26 15	Skipton	A	9-29
		D	9-31
36 16	Hellifield	A	9W49
		D	9W54
39 36	Settle Junct.		9-59
46 74	Clapham		10-16
54 32	Wennington Junc.		10-32
63 60	Carnforth East Junc.		10-44
64 00	Carnforth F. & M. Junc.	A	10-45
		D	10-48
64 38	Carnforth No. 2 Junc.	A	10-51
		D	10-53
64 43	Carnforth Station	A	10-54
		D	10-56
77 31	Oxenholme		11-11
90 32	Tebay		11-26
95 68	Shap Summit		11-35
	Penrith No. 1		11-48
109 43	Penrith	A	11-49

Change engine

M. Ch.	Station		p.m.
113 28	Blencow		12-05
117 16	Penruddock		12-15
124 22	Threlkeld		12-23
127 57	Keswick		12-38
130 09	Braithwaite		12-43
135 05	Bassenthwaite Lake		12-51
140 13	Cockermouth	A	12-56
		D	1-04
140 78	Cockermouth Junc.		1-06

M. Ch.	Station		p.m.
148 51	Derwent Junc.		1-21
149 07	Workington Main	A	1-23
0 00	Workington Main	D	2-20
9 06	Cockermouth		2-39
22 50	Keswick		3-09
40 36	Penrith		3-50
58 16	Carlisle	A	4-40
	Change engine		
		D	5-30
0 59	Carlisle No. 3		5-32
1 32	Canal Junc.		5-34
9 38	Drumburgh	A	5-52
		D	5-55
22 16	Silloth	A	6-12
		D	6-32
34 74	Drumburgh	A	6-49
43 00	Canal Junc.	D	7-04
43 53	Carlisle No. 3		7-06
44 32	Carlisle	A	7-08
	Change engine		
		D	7-25
45 24	Petteril Bridge Junc.		7-28
59 70	Lazonby & Kirkoswald		7-50
75 17	Appleby West		8-10
92 62	Ais Gill		8-40
103 77	Blea Moor	A	8-53
117 77	Settle Junct.	D	9-06
121 17	Hellifield	A	9-10
		D	9-12
131 18	Skipton	A	9-31
132 32	Snaygill	D	9-34
140 33	Keighley		9-42
146 56	Shipley Leeds Junc.	A	9-49
157 33	Leeds City South	D	10-05

Total Steam mileage - 364 m. 64 ch.

Total D.M.U. mileage - 80 m. 6 ch.

Mileage—Steam to Whitehaven, D.M.U. to Carlisle, etc. - 386 m. 46 ch.

DIESEL MULTIPLE UNIT

M. Ch.	Station		p.m.
0 0	Workington Main	D	1-38
1 41	Moss Bay Iron Works		1-41
6 56	Whitehaven Bransty		1-53
8 02	Corkickle		1-56
11 15	Moor Row		2-03
16 41	Rowrah	A	2-23
		D	2-38
21 67	Moor Row	A	2-58
		D	3-03
24 15	Egremont		3-12
26 09	Beckermet Mines Junc.		3-18
29 33	Sellafield	A	3-26
		D	3-41

M. Ch.	Station		p.m.
32 75	Nethertown		3-47
35 58	St. Bees		3-52
38 77	Corkickle		3-59
40 23	Whitehaven Bransty		4-02
45 38	Moss Bay Iron Works		4-14
46 79	Workington Main		4-16
52 42	Maryport		4-23
59 79	Aspatria		4-34
68 35	Wigton		4-44
79 11	Carlisle No. 8		4-55
80 06	Carlisle	A	4-58

EXPECTED MOTIVE POWER

LEEDS	—	PENRITH	—	M.N. PACIFIC
PENRITH	—	WORKINGTON	—	IVATT 2-6-0
CARLISLE	—	SILLOTH	—	SCOTTISH PRESERVED LOCOS
CARLISLE	—	LEEDS	—	M.N. PACIFIC
WORKINGTON	—	SELLAFIELD	—	CARLISLE — D.M.U.

gain time as we departed from Carlisle 20 minutes late.

We left in grand style and passed Armathwaite at 70 mph, but permanent way slowings at Long Marton and Culgaith meant that we took 42 min 2 sec to Appleby, which was passed at 54 mph. What followed, however, was quite outstanding, as we were still not really going very fast at Ormside. I don't think the Holbeck driver had ever known such progress up the 1 in 100, and I have never seen a fireman work as hard. The end result was that the 17.45 miles from Appleby to the summit were covered in 17 min 41 sec, an average of 59.58 mph.

Details of the speeds are given in the accompanying table, as published in the *Railway Observer*. I remember the conductor warning the crew to take water at the troughs at Garsdale, but of course this was not possible with a 'Merchant Navy' (no water

troughs on the Southern), so they carried on, past Blea Moor and on to Hellifield. We were stopped at Settle Junction, and there was much concern about the lack of water, so the engine was worked very easily to Hellifield, where the water column was a most welcome sight to the crew. After all this excitement, the journey to Leeds was taken at a more sedate pace.

It really was a fantastic performance, considering that the crew had been on duty since about 7.30 am and did not get back to Leeds until after 10 pm.

Since the return to steam on the Settle and Carlisle line, there have been many epic climbs from Appleby to Ais Gill with the 'Duchess', 'A4s', an 'A2', and so on, but with crews that had started from Carlisle, and with a fully prepared engine from Appleby, so comparison is not really fair.

So ended what was arguably the finest of the West Riding branch tours.

	Miles	Speed
Carlisle (dep)	0.00	
Petteril Bridge Junction	3.22	
Scotby	7.04	39
Cumwhinton	8.55	46/58/70
Armathwaite	15.17	70
Lazonby	21.03	69/73$^{1}/_{2}$
Little Salkeld	23.30	71
Culgaith	30.00	23
Newbiggin	33.20	34/46/25
Long Marton	38.15	46/51
Appleby	42.02	54/64/72
Ormside	44.11	66$^{1}/_{2}$/55
Crosby Garrett	49.20	62/64
Kirkby Stephen	52.17	60/53
Mallerstang	55.47	57/50
Ais Gill	59.43	50/66
Garsdale	62.39	61/64
Dent	65.44	66$^{1}/_{2}$/70
Blea Moor	70.38	58/65
Ribblehead	71.57	65/72
Selside	74.02	72$^{1}/_{2}$/76
Horton	75.51	80/64 (eased)
Helwith Bridge	77.08	66$^{1}/_{2}$/75
Settle Junc (arr)	83.04	

Driver Bert Hooker and fireman Ken Seaby pose with No 35012. I am sure they were looking forward to the outing even more than the passengers, and it was probably one of the most memorable of their careers. Their efforts made the tour one of the best remembered of all the West Riding branch specials, although fireman Seaby said he was glad he didn't have to work as hard every day on the Southern as he did between Appleby and Ais Gill summit! *Gavin Morrison*

Ready to depart from Leeds City on the famous outing is rebuilt 'Merchant Navy' No 35012 *United States Lines*. Built in January 1945 as No 21C12, it was renumbered in March 1949, and rebuilt in February 1957. No 35012 was withdrawn three months before the end of steam on the Southern, in April 1967, having covered 1,134,836, the fourth highest mileage by any member of the class. Regrettably, despite so many members of the class having been preserved, *United States Lines* is not included, being scrapped by J. H. Cashmore of Newport. *Gavin Morrison*

Above left The Control Office on the West Coast Main Line over Shap always seemed to manage to send a slow freight or DMU out in front of our West Riding branch specials, and ruin spectacular performances. No 35012 is seen here just after restarting the special at Shap Wells on the 1 in 75 gradient. *Rodney Lissenden*

Left Well-groomed Ivatt 2-6-0s Nos 46426 and 46458 pass Bassenthwaite Lake station heading for Workington. This section of line from Keswick to Workington was to close in April 1966, whilst the remainder from Penrith to Keswick section finished on 6 March 1972. Much of the line has since been incorporated into the realigned A66 road. *Gavin Morrison*

Above The line to Silloth closed on 7 September 1964, less than three months after the Solway Ranger tour. Two Scottish preserved locomotives headed the special, which is seen after arrival, with Great North of Scotland 4-4-0 No 49 (BR number 62277) *Gordon Highlander* leading. The locomotive was withdrawn in 1958, then repainted into the GNofS green livery. Behind is the famous Caledonian 'Single' No 123, whose exploits in the 'Races to the North' of the 1880s and '90s have been well documented. Built by Neilson & Co in 1886, it was withdrawn in 1935 and kept at St Rollox Works until reinstated to traffic in 1957. Both locomotives are now in the Glasgow Transport Museum. *Gavin Morrison*

United States Line sets off from Carlisle on its epic run over the Settle and Carlisle line, beautifully lit by the evening sun. *John Hirst*

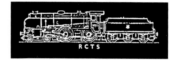

Saturday 27 June 1964
The High Peak Rail Tour

This tour was organised by the Sheffield branch, and it was appropriate that the Woodhead route, together with the Cromford & High Peak lines, should be selected as the main features.

Class 'B1' No 61360 turned out to be the train engine and the tour departed on time from Sheffield Victoria. It began by heading east and turning left at Woodburn Junction, through Tinsley Yard, Rotherham and Masborough to Wath. Here the prototype electric 'EM1' No 26000 *Tommy* was attached to pilot the train to Penistone. The 'B1' was shut off and the electric hauled it and the train up the famous Worsborough Bank. A spirited run to Guide Bridge with a maximum of 67 mph at Torside had the train well on time until it was blocked by a late-running Sheffield to Manchester train which was allowed to proceed in front to Guide Bridge.

There Stockport Edgeley men took over, and after trying to gain some time more delays meant that Stockport was passed 26 minutes late. In spite of poor weather conditions the locomotive gave a reasonable performance to Buxton, where a pilotman was taken on board for the journey to Parsley Hay. Fortunately the rain ceased for the run in open wagons over the Cromford & High Peak line - passengers on some tours in the past had received a real soaking at this location!

'J94s' Nos 68012 and 68079 were the predictable motive power to Middleton Top, where the winding

engine was inspected. Kitson 0-4-0ST No 47006 was on duty on the second level to Sheep Pasture. A further 'J94', No 68006, did the final short journey from Cromford to High Peak Junction, where the 'B1' was ready to carry on back to Sheffield.

The return trip followed a devious route via Butterley, Pye Bridge and the Mansfield branch of the Midland. Water was taken at Mansfield Town, and some new diesels were noted on passing Shirebrook. A 25-minute delay then occurred until a relief crew arrived on a 'WD' at Elmton and Cresswell. The tour eventually arrived at Sheffield Victoria at 20.11, some 17 minutes late. Thus the tour was completed, having provided an interesting day out, and being well supported.

The special passes Penistone, in the days when it was an important junction, Class 'EM1' No 26000 *Tommy* piloting 'B1' No 61360. No 26000 had an interesting history. Built in 1947 and numbered No 6701 as the prototype 1500-volt electric locomotive, it was re-numbered 6000 by the LNER and was then loaned to the Netherlands State Railways to provide operating experience on the locomotive, and to help with a motive power shortage. It returned in 1952 and was then renumbered to No 26000 in the British Railways sequence. It was withdrawn in April 1970. *Gavin Morrison*

It was on 10 April 1956 that 'J94' No 68030 was first tested on the upper section of the Cromford & High Peak line between Middleton Top and Parsley Hay. The 0-6-0T North London tanks were past their best and in August 1956 Nos 68006 and 68013 joined 68030. Other members of the class arrived between 1959 and 1962. Looking distinctly the worse for wear, Nos 68079 and 68012 are seen at Middleton Top with the open wagons. The 'J94s' survived to the end of the line in April 1967. *Gavin Morrison*

No 61360, allocated to Doncaster, approaches Parsley Hay before transferring the passengers to the open wagons for the trip over the Cromford & High Peak line. This loco-motive was built by the North British Locomotive Co in March 1949 and was withdrawn in April 1966. *Gavin Morrison*

Saturday 26 September 1964
The Scottish Lowlander

This was another classic Lancashire and North West branch tour.

It is said that hindsight is a wonderful thing, and if ever there was a tour I should have travelled on rather than photographed, this was it! But the temptation to have one last picture of a 'Duchess' at Shap was too much. As it turned out the pictures were poor and the locomotive performances superb.

This was of course the day that many of the passengers were dreading or could not believe, as it was to be the last trip of a 'Duchess' over Shap. The speed with which the class was withdrawn caught many by surprise, many locomotives still being in good order, but the branch decided that the sad event must not go without some tribute, so The Scottish Lowlander tour was planned. It was appropriate that the locomotive should be No 46256 *Sir William Stanier FRS*, which was only 17 years old and was about to be withdrawn!

Once again hopes were high of a fast run to Carlisle, but as on so many trips Control on the West Coast line did not get it quite right and the passengers were treated to some brilliant moments rather than an overall good trip.

Details of the journey are reproduced from the report in the *Railway Observer*. The load was around 450 tons gross, which was appropriate. The Preston crew, probably well known to many of the RCTS members, really gave the loco its head after a perma-

nent way slack at milepost 29½, resulting in Tebay being passed at 60 mph and the summit at 38 mph in 6¾ minutes.

Whether by design or accident, it was a nice touch to see 'A4' No 60007 *Sir Nigel Gresley* from Ferryhill depot waiting to take the train forward to Edinburgh over the Waverley route.

It is ironic that the tour was to commemorate the 'Duchesses', for as it turned out it was really the 'A4' that produced the highlight of the day.

The 450-ton load was heavy for the Waverley line, and there were those on board who believed that the 'A4s' were for flying up and down the East Coast Main Line with much lighter trains, and it was Stanier's masterpieces that were the real power machines. However, the timings reproduced in the accompanying table were so fantastic that had it not been a railtour, anybody claiming such times when on his own would have had difficulty in making them believed.

The crew was driver Maclaren and fireman Whiteman from Kingmoor, and a net time of 58.5 minutes from Carlisle to Hawick must certainly be a record with a train of this weight. The locomotive was in its latter years, and not in the condition it used to be when at King's Cross, but this was one of the finest performances ever produced and recorded with this famous engine - but maybe the famous Bill Hoole of King's Cross knew differently.

At Niddrie West Junction *Sir Nigel Gresley* was exchanged for the famous Haymarket 'A4' *Union of South Africa*, and while the locomotive performed well back via the Glasgow & South Western line, the driver kept to the overall 75 mph limit in Scotland, so after No 60007's performance it was bound to be a slight anti-climax.

The grand finale of the 'Duchesses' had finally arrived as *Sir William Stanier FRS* set off south from Carlisle 12 minutes late, which was just enough to encourage the crew to give a fine climb. As the magnificent red machine forged its way to the summit with its 450-ton load in 38¾ minutes, a time which was as good as when they were in their prime, it was hard to believe that once the fire was dropped at Crewe North shed later than night it was the end for the famous locomotives.

Princess Coronation Class 4-6-2 No. 46256 *Sir William A. Stanier, F.R.S.*					
PRESTON-CARLISLE					
Saturday, 26th September, 1964					
Driver Johnson, Fireman White (Preston Shed)					
Miles				Sched.	Actual	Speeds
0.0	Preston	..	..	0	0.00	
9.5	Garstang	..	..	13	11.47	74/70
					sig. check	
21.0	Lancaster	..	..	23	23.05	20
24.9	..	..	..		sig. stop	
27.3	Carnforth	..	..	28	32.04	55/62
34.5	Milnthorpe	..	..		39.04	72
40.1	Oxenholme	..	..	43	44.36	52/54
47.1	Grayrigg	..	..		53.29	42 (min.)
50.5	*Milepost 29¼*	..		p.w.s.	25
53.1	Tebay	..	..	59	61.27	60
54.5	Tebay North I.B.S.				62.49	61
56.1	Scout Green Crossing				64.38	48
58.7	Shap Summit	..		69	68.14	38 (min.)
					sig. stops	
90.1	Carlisle	..	..	104	108.56	
Net Time: 90¼ minutes.						
Approx. equivalent draw bar horse power at Tebay North: 2400.						

Once passed Shap Summit the usual West Coast delays occurred, resulting in a 14¹/₂ minutes late arrival at Preston, a poor reward for the crew who had gained over 5 minutes from Carlisle to Shap Summit. But for many participants the West Coast Main Line could never be quite the same again.

The Waverley route is now history, as, unfortunately, is *Sir William Stanier FRS*, but on the brighter side the two 'A4s' are still with us and still thrilling those who knew them in BR days, as well as the younger generation. In addition, *Duchess of Hamilton*, with its exploits over the Settle and Carlisle line and other routes, has given many demonstrations of what the locomotives were capable of doing. Saturday 26 September 1964 has so far proved to be the last occasion when a 'Duchess' worked between Preston and Carlisle on the West Coast Main Line.

Passing the remains of Grayrigg station, closed on 1 February 1954, *Sir William Stanier FRS*, travelling, according to the log in the *Railway Observer*, at 42 mph, reaches the summit of the bank on the Scottish Lowlander's journey north. *Howard Malham*

Whilst the tour participants were enjoying the performances of the 'A4s' through Scotland, No 46256 was being prepared in the fading light on Upperby depot, ready for its last trip back to Crewe. *Gavin Morrison*

Another view of *Sir William Stanier FRS* on Carlisle Upperby depot. *Gavin Morrison*

The historic change-over at Carlisle, when for the last time *Sir William Stanier FRS* is shown ready to take over from one of the famous Scottish 'A4s', *Union of South Africa*. Carlisle was probably the only station in the country where in the past the two rival 'Pacifics' could be seen side by side. *Howard Malham*

9 and 16 January 1965
Derwent Valley Light Railway Tour

This was another West Riding Branch Special. Mid-January was in hindsight not the best month to have had a tour in unheated coaches, but in spite of the coolish conditions a good time was had by all. This was also not a day to bother bringing your stop-watch, since the motive power was Class '03' diesel shunter No D2111.

The two tours turned out to be the last excursions to run on the line, except for some tourist trains run from 1977 to 1979 with preserved 'J72' No 69023 *Joem*, which in fact were not a success.

The outward trip took nearly 2³/₄ hours with lengthy stops at every station. Passenger services ceased as long ago as August 1926, when even rail-cars could not pay their way, but freight lingered on until finally ending in September 1981.

The accompanying photographs show views of the special at some of the stations *en route*.

Ready to depart from Layerthorpe at York. *Gavin Morrison*

One of the line's distinctive stations, at Dinnington. *Gavin Morrison*

Another photo-stop, this time at Wheldrake. *Gavin Morrison*

Ready to depart from Thorganby. *Gavin Morrison*

Journey's end at Cliff Common. The Class '03' shunter prepares to run round the train. *Gavin Morrison*

Saturday 13 February 1965
Rebuilt Scot Commemorative Rail Tour

A good number of the tours organised in the mid-1960s were in many ways rather sad occasions, being often last trips of classes with which many of us had grown up, and which had been pat of our lives.

This tour, organised by the Lancashire and North West branch, was conceived on the basis of it being the last with a rebuilt 'Scot', but as things turned out a few of the class did survive until later in the year, due, it was said, to a shortage of Class 7 power on the LM area.

This shortage of power seemed to be the cry of all sheds. I well remember at Holbeck hearing the foreman saying that he had no power for a certain train, and the shed yard and roundhouses were full of Class '5s' or similar machines. Kingmoor was another depot which always seemed to be full of locomotives.

The locomotive for the tour was to have been No

THE
RAILWAY CORRESPONDENCE
AND TRAVEL SOCIETY

46145 Duke of Wellington's Regiment (West Riding)
approaching Ais Gill summit with the up Waverley.

ITINERARY OF THE
REBUILT SCOT COMMEMORATIVE
RAILTOUR

Saturday, 13th February, 1965

Tour organised by the Lancashire and North West Branch

46160 *Queen's Westminster Rifleman*, a Longsight (9A) engine for many years, but it had failed and was on Holbeck shed, so No 46115 *Scots Guardsman* was substituted, again for a long time a Longsight loco. It was also the first rebuilt 'Scot' to be fitted with deflectors; but they were handsome machines, with or without them. To the great credit of Crewe North Depot, the far from ex-works loco was really cleaned up, and looked very smart for the tour, together with plywood nameplates.

The rebuilt Scots had suffered a miserable demise, working freights and secondary passenger trains, and externally most looked terrible. Mechanically *Scots Guardsman* was in reasonable condition, though not a very good steamer, but the schedule was leisurely.

The train was a ten-coach formation for the 450 passengers, and the route from Crewe was down the main line to Boars Head and on to Blackburn, then to Hellifield. A 55-minute break was taken to allow the passengers to visit Hellifield Depot, which was then under the control of the Curator of the Museum of British Transport, a Mr Scholes, and contained a wide variety of locomotives which had been selected for preservation, the most noticeable being 'V2' No 4771 *Green Arrow*, together with the 'J17', the two North Eastern Electric locos, Nos 26500/1, and others. This was the first visit that had been allowed, and was sanctioned by the Curator, and Mr Dow of LM Stoke office (the father of the current Keeper of the National Railway Museum, York).

The Crewe North driver and fireman said that they would do their best to give a good climb to Blea Moor and on to Carlisle, the Settle and Carlisle line having been home to the rebuilt 'Scots' from 1943 to 1965 on the Scottish expresses.

A stop had to be made for water at Settle as the Hellifield column was out of action, so there was no run at the bank. None the less, the locomotives had always been strong machines rather than fast runners, although one is believed to have achieved 100 mph between Penrith and Carlisle, and I have heard many unsubstantiated tales about 100 mph speeds down the banks from Blea Moor and Ais Gill. A perfect start was made from Settle on the 1 in 100 climb to Blea Moor, and lost time was regained, with further gains to Carlisle.

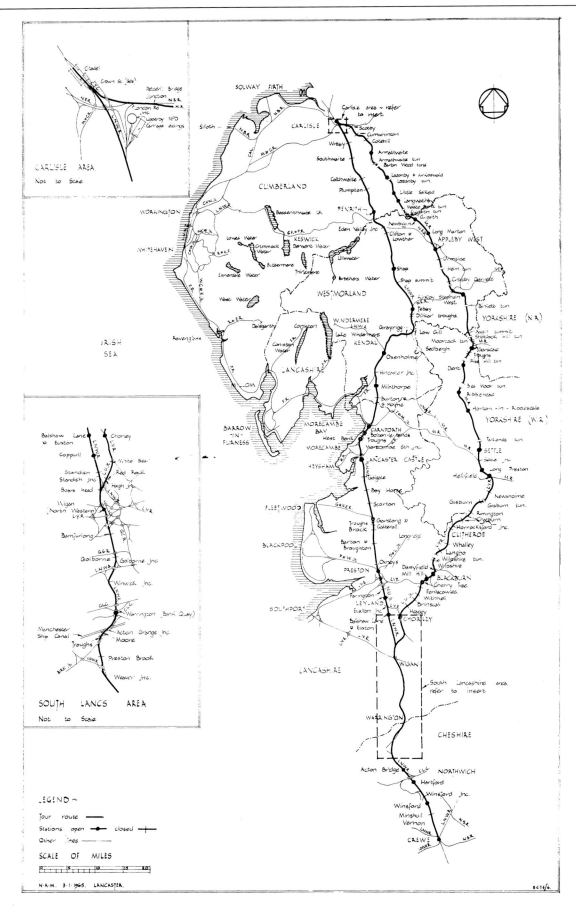

CARLISLE AREA.
Not to Scale

SOUTH LANCS AREA
Not to Scale

LEGEND ~
Tour route ————
Stations open ●—● closed ✝
Other lines ————

SCALE OF MILES

A break of 1¹/₂ hours was allowed at Carlisle before the train headed south. For various reasons, mainly permanent way slacks, as mentioned elsewhere, the LMR could not give the special an uninterrupted run to Shap, although a time of 17 min 9 sec from Penrith to the summit was excellent; as was pointed out in the *Railway Observer* report, the time was only 1 minute outside the schedule for the old 'Caledonian' with a 'Duchess' and a load of 280 tons. From Shap Summit the run back to Crewe was uneventful.

A few other members of the class lingered on for a month or two, and as it turned out *Scots Guardsman* was the last to be withdrawn, in January 1966. Fortunately it was preserved, but over the years has had a rather chequered history. During its long stay at Dinting it was put into working order and given permission to run on about three occasions. It is currently at the Birmingham Museum at Tyseley, need-

ing a large amount of money to be spent on it to get its main-line certificate. Of all the miracles that have been performed by the preservation movement, the job of getting *Scots Guardsman* back on the main line to work the Settle and Carlisle route must be one of the most important yet to be achieved.

This tour was for many of the passengers their last run behind a rebuilt 'Scot'. Sad though the occasion may have been, a good day out was had by all, with perfect weather.

Right A fine portrait taken during the break at Hellifield, showing the well turned out rebuilt 'Scot' No 46115 *Scots Guardsman*.

All the class were rebuilt, starting with No 6103 *Royal Scots Fusilier* in 1943, and finishing with No 46137 *Prince of Wales' Volunteers (South Lancashire)* in 1955. Five of the class were regular performers over the Settle and Carlisle line from the mid-1940s until 1960 - these were Nos 46103/08/09/17/33, allocated to Holbeck depot at Leeds. Nos 46113, 46130 and 46145 joined them later. *Gavin Morrison*

DIMENSIONS

	Rebuilt Scot	Rebuilt Patriot	British Legion
Cylinders (3)	18″ x 26″	17″ x 26″	18″ x 26″
Driving wheel diameter	6′9″	6′9″	6′9″
Boiler			
Pressure	250lb/sq.in.	250lb/sq.in.	250lb/sq.in.
Large tubes (outside dia.)	28 x 5⅛″	28 x 5⅛″	28 x 5⅛″
Small tubes (outside dia.)	198 x 1¾″	198 x 1¾″	180 x 1⅞″
Superheater elements (outside dia.)	28 x 1¼″	28 x 1¼″	28 x 1¼″
Grate area	31.25 sq.ft.	31.25 sq.ft.	31.25 sq.ft.
Total heating surface	2,210 sq.ft.	2,210 sq.ft.	2,336 sq.ft.
Tractive effort	33,150 lbs.	29,590 lbs.	33,150 lbs
Weight of engine	83T.OC.	82T.OC.	84T.1C.
Length of engine	39′ 9¼″	39′ 7″	40′ 1″

The Stanier round-topped 4000 gallon tender was the standard fitting on the rebuilds.

SCHEDULE

OUTWARD

Mls. Ch.			Sched. Times
0.00	CREWE	dep.	9.15
16.21	Weaver Jct.	pass	9.33
24.10	Warrington B. Q.	pass	9.42
35.70	WIGAN N. W.	arr.	9.57
		dep.	10.02
41.51	Adlington Jct.	pass	10.15
44.27	Chorley	pass	10.21
54.07	BLACKBURN	arr.	10.45
		dep.	10.55
64.72	Clitheroe	pass	11.15
78.31	HELLIFIELD	arr.	11.35
		dep.	12.30
81.50	Settle Jct.	pass	12.36
95.58	Blea Moor	pass	13.06
106.76	Ais Gill	pass	13.26
124.31	Appleby West	pass	13.50
156.08	CARLISLE (C.)	arr.	14.28

RETURN

Mls. Ch.			Sched. Times
0.00	CARLISLE (C.)	dep.	16.05
12.78	Plumpton	pass	16.28
17.69	Penrith	pass	16.35
31.44	Shap Summit	pass	17.03
37.00	Tebay	pass	17.09
50.01	Oxenholme	pass	17.22
62.69	Carnforth	pass	17.35
69.08	Lancaster (C.)	pass	17.42
80.49	Garstang	pass	17.59
90.07	PRESTON	arr.	18.15
		dep.	18.19
95.45	Euxton Jct.	pass	18.27
105.17	WIGAN N. W.	arr.	18.40
		dep.	18.44
116.77	Warrington B. Q.	pass	18.59
124.66	Weaver Jct.	pass	19.07
141.07	CREWE	arr.	19.30

Another view of the locomotive at Hellifield. Note the yellow stripe on the cab side indicating it was banned from operating on the West Coast Main Line South of Crewe. *Gavin Morrison*

Scots Guardsman approaches Ribblehead station on its way to Carlisle. The line off to the right served the quarry. *Gavin Morrison*

Sunday 21 March 1965
The Tyne-Solway Rail Tour

By the standards of previous West Riding branch tours, this one was decidedly unspectacular - in fact, I would go as far as to say that it was the most unexciting and uninteresting railtour on which I travelled. However, it does serve to demonstrate that not *all* the outings provided 'fireworks'. To be fair to the committee it was organised at very short notice, to replace a South Yorkshire tour which had got into difficulties. The motive power was 'A1' 'Pacific' No 60131 *Osprey*, for many years allocated to Copley Hill for the Leeds-King's Cross expresses, but now in a rather run-down condition. With very little work it was usually to be found for most of the week at either Holbeck or Neville Hill depots awaiting the call to take over from a failed diesel, which by 1965 was not very often. The load for the tour was a meagre six coaches, which had the schedule required it could have produced some lively running, but it was not to be.

The weather did its worst; we were greeted by a

considerable snowfall when we rose in the morning, so much so that some passengers failed to get to Leeds, and this of course raised speculation as to what the weather would be like over the Settle and Carlisle line on the return journey.

We departed from Leeds promptly at 9.55 am in almost a blizzard and headed north, but by the time Harrogate was passed it was raining, and by Ripon the sun was out with not a hint of snow anywhere.

Time was kept on the easy schedule to Stockton where water was taken, and we proceeded at a very leisurely pace to West Hartlepool. Between there and Sunderland the schedule changed from the lethargic to the impossible; we dropped 10 minutes and did not regain anything to Gateshead, where the party detrained for a visit to the depot, which was full of diesels, although an 'A1' was also present.

The weather was dull and cold and the party returned to the station to rejoin the train, which unfortunately hadn't arrived. Difficulty in finding an operable water column in Newcastle Central was the problem, resulting in a 30 minutes late departure for Carlisle.

George Stephenson's cottage was observed as we headed west, and we were travelling along quite well until stopped at Haydon Bridge. A rumour started that the halt was due to sheep on the line, but this was incorrect. It was just that we had caught up with a local DMU in a very long section, so this cost a further 12 minutes - but at least the passengers had an extra photo-stop. Carlisle was eventually reached at 16.20, 56 minutes late, and the locomotive departed for Kingmoor to be serviced.

Some time was saved at Carlisle, and we left there at 17.02, now only 40 minutes late, a fine opportunity for an 'A1' and six coaches to really set forth past Durran Hill. Initially progress was good, but after Appleby speed dropped badly due to the fire not having been cleaned properly at Kingmoor, and a poor climb to Ais Gill resulted - 58 minutes non-stop with an 'A1' on a six-coach train was not very exciting.

There is little else to say about the rest of the trip. The tour eventually arrived back in Leeds 30 minutes late, which was due to the easy schedule rather than the performance of the locomotive, and so ended a rather unspectacular day out.

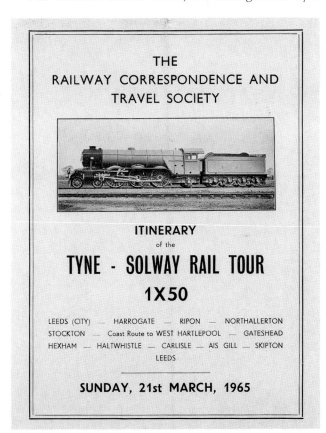

THE
RAILWAY CORRESPONDENCE AND
TRAVEL SOCIETY

ITINERARY
of the
TYNE - SOLWAY RAIL TOUR
1X50

LEEDS (CITY) — HARROGATE — RIPON — NORTHALLERTON
STOCKTON — Coast Route to WEST HARTLEPOOL — GATESHEAD
HEXHAM — HALTWHISTLE — CARLISLE — AIS GILL — SKIPTON
LEEDS

SUNDAY, 21st MARCH, 1965

Right Branch committee member Don Southgate strides down the snow-covered platform at Leeds with the RCTS headboard to place it on 'A1' No 60131 *Osprey*. The 'A1' was a local West Riding locomotive for 12 of its 17 years, spending most of its time at Copley Hill working the King's Cross express. A batch of 'A1s' were transferred to Neville Hill in July 1963 for around two years before withdrawal, but saw very little use, being mainly standby locomotives for expresses working north of Leeds. They did, however, have a regular summer Saturday diagram over the Settle and Carlisle line to Glasgow on the CTAC tours train. Cleaning of the locomotive must have been rushed, as no white paint had been applied to the numberplate and shedplate. The locomotive was built at Darlington in June 1950 and was withdrawn a few months after the tour, in October 1965. *Gavin Morrison*

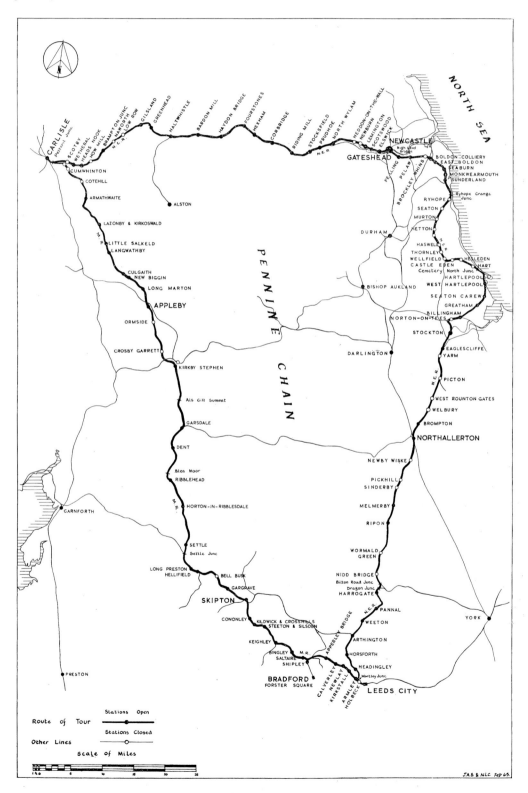

The crew of *Osprey* pose for a picture in the comfort of their cab, before heading north for Northallerton and Newcastle. In the centre is Holbeck Inspector Albert Pullen, a well-known character around Leeds for many years, who accompanied many of the West Riding branch tours. *Gavin Morrison*

SCHEDULE

Miles					Miles				
0.00	LEEDS CITY	S.	D	09.55	109.14	Scotswood		Pass	14.00
0.76	Wortley Jnc.		Pass	09.59	115.48	West Wylam	—	,,	14.12
9.23	Arthington	—	,,	10.14	127.26	Hexham —	—	,,	14.28
18.22	Harrogate	—	,,	10.29	143.52	Haltwhistle	—	,,	14.50
29.59	Ripon —	—	,,	10.47	155.59	Brampton Jnc.	—	,,	15.06
43.40	Northallerton	—	,,	11.05	166.57	Carlisle —	—	A	15.24
58.14	Eaglescliffe	—	,,	11.25				D	16.22
61.17	Stockton —	—	A	11.31	182.15	Lazonby —		Pass	16.56
	(W)		D	11.37	197.42	Appleby West	—	,,	17.03
72.68	W. Hartlepool		Pass	11.55	215.07	Ais Gill —	—	,,	17.30
85.01	Haswell —	—	,,	12.15	226.22	Blea Moor	—	,,	17.42
94.27	Sunderland	—	,,	12.26	240.22	Settle Jnc.	—	,,	17.55
102.79	Pelaw —	—	,,	12.40	243.22	Hellifield—	—	,,	17.58
105.74	Gateshead	East	A	12.50	253.43	Skipton —	—	A	18.10
		West	D	13.50		(W)		D	18.14
106.16	Newcastle	—	A	13.53	262.58	Keighley —		Pass	18.27
			D	13.55	269.01	Shipley/Leeds Jnc.		,,	18.37
					279.58	Leeds City S.	—	A	18.56

Skipton	—	D	18.20
Keighley	—	D	18.36
Shipley	—	A	18.46
Bradford	—	A	18.53

All the snow encountered at Leeds had vanished by Ripon. The tour was booked to stop at Stockton for the locomotive to take water, as shown here. Note the station's lovely overall roof, which was later removed. *Gavin Morrison*

Sunday 19 September 1965
The Blyth Tyne Tour

The mid-1960s were producing more RCTS-organised railtours per annum than at any other time, and there were plenty of good reasons for running them: last of classes, closing lines, steam on routes which were now dieselised, and so on. The RCTS ran 15 tours during the year, which represented a terrific amount of work by the various committees.

The West Riding branch had requested an 'A4' for this tour, which presented some difficulty as the eight remaining members of the class were allocated to Ferryhill depot at Aberdeen, except for No 60031 *Golden Plover* which was at St Rollox at Glasgow, but was withdrawn the following month. Never the less, British Rail did not disappoint the 381 passengers, as No 60004 *William Whitelaw* was worked down for the occasion. The locomotive had been transferred to Haymarket depot at Edinburgh in 1941 where it remained until being moved to

Left Inspector Geoff Wilson, who accompanied many of the West Riding branch tours in the 1960s, leaning out of the cab of 'A4' No 60004 *William Whitelaw* at Eaglescliffe, before working light engine to Darlington depot for servicing. *Gavin Morrison*

Right William Whitelaw blows its chime whistle as it approaches Bishop Auckland under the impressive signal gantry. The locomotive was originally named *Great Snipe* and numbered 4462, but was renamed in July 1941. Built in November 1937, it survived until July 1966, and was always associated with Haymarket depot in Edinburgh, although it did have short spells at King's Cross, Gateshead and Heaton before moving to Scotland in July 1941; it remained at Haymarket depot for 21 years. *Gavin Morrison*

Aberdeen Ferryhill around 1963.

William Whitelaw brought the empty stock in from Neville Hill sidings to Leeds City, where the special departed 3 minutes late with a Neville Hill Crew plus myself and our regular inspector on the footplate.

A gentle climb to Bramhope Tunnel was made due to the rails being rather slippery, so we were 5 minutes late as we passed non-stop through Harrogate, but a good performance to Northallerton got us back on time. We then travelled on to Eaglescliffe, where the sun shone for a photo-stop.

The 'A4' was detached, and English Electric Type 3 No D6769, still active today as No 37079, backed on to the train to take us to Darlington over the Stockton & Darlington direct line through Fighting Cocks; the state of the track was not apparently fit for the 'A4', which meanwhile went to Darlington shed for service.

A visit to Darlington Works was a feature of the tour, and it was pleasing to see steam locomotives still receiving general repairs in the form of 'Austerity' 2-8-0s, Stanier 2-8-0s and a North Eastern 'Q6'.

William Whitelaw rejoined the train at Darlington and took us by an indirect route to Newcastle via Shildon, Bishop Auckland and Willington, joining the main line again at Relly Mill Junction. A fast trip to Newcastle from passing Durham resulted in a 6-minute early arrival.

The 'A4' left the train again at Newcastle and was replaced by Ivatt 2-6-0 No 43057, which took us on a tour of the Riverside branch, Percy Main, Mewsham, Bedlington and on to the main line at Morpeth, where there was a photographic stop. We then headed via Cramlington viaduct, Forest Hill curve and South Gosforth to Newcastle Central and Blaydon, where the train reversed and returned via Derwenthaugh and Gateshead to Pelaw, where our 'A4' was waiting.

There were problems with the Ivatt during this part of the trip, which I seem to remember were due to the crew being upset about something, which resulted in a 36 minutes late departure. We headed through Wakington and Ferryhill to Norton Junction where further time was lost, as there were main-line diversions in progress and we had lost our path.

We eventually joined the main line again at Croft Spa, and hopes were high of a fast run to York. However, nothing spectacular resulted, as speed did not exceed 72 mph, nothing very special for an 'A4' on this 'racetrack'.

Eventually we arrived back at Leeds 46 minutes behind schedule, but a good day had once again been enjoyed. For many of the passengers this was probably their last trip behind an 'A4' in BR ownership.

The special crosses the fine viaduct out of Bishop Auckland *en route* to Newcastle. *Hugh Ballantyne*

Ivatt '4MT' 2-6-0 No 43057 takes the train over the viaduct between Beeside and Bedlington. Built at Doncaster in 1950, the locomotive was withdrawn in 1966. *Hugh Ballantyne*

Saturday 23 October 1965
South Yorkshire No 5 Rail Tour

This tour was carefully designed to cover many freight lines in South Yorkshire, an area which still had a high density of railways. The accompanying map and timings show in detail the route followed.

The weather was bad, with visibility no more than 100 yards, and dirty local Stanier '8F' No 48202 from Mirfield was also a disappointment, but with our regular inspector on board, Geoff Wilson, the train set forth from Leeds Central. At Low Moor the train was wrongly signalled on to the Halifax line instead of the Cleckheaton branch, which involved a short reversal.

The weather continued to be dismal, and around Manvers Main Colliery the visibility was terrible, but nevertheless the train arrived at Wrangbrook Junction on the old Hull & Barnsley line roughly on time, where the '8F' was exchanged for Brush Type 2 diesel No D5561, which became Class 31 No 31143.

There was plenty to look at from the train, although much of it was rather depressing, as disused lines

ROUTE AND TIMES

M. Ch.				
00 00	Leeds Central	—	09.15	
00 41	Holbeck High Level		09.17	
07 33	Laisterdyke —		09.37	
09 24	Bowling Jnc.	—	09.43	
10 79	Low Moor —	—	09.48	
15 54	Heckmondwike Jnc.		09.57	
18 16	Thornhill Jnc.	—	10.05	
19 25	Midland Jnc.	—	10.10	
22 70	Horbury Jnc.	—	10.15	
25 13	WAKEFIELD			
	(Kirkgate)	A	10.20	
		D	10.26	
26 71	Croften West Jnc.	—	10.31	
28 20	Hare Park Jnc.	—	10.35	
34 14	S. Kirkby Jnc.	—	10.50	
34 75	Moorthorpe —		10.55	
40 76	Dearne Jnc. —		11.05	
41 63	Wath Jnc. —		11.08	
47 19	Stairfoot	—A	11.20	
		D	11.22	
50 44	Cudworth Yd. Sth.	—	11.29	
51 00	Cudworth Yd. Nth.	—A	11.30	
		D	12.15	
58 46	Wrangbrook—	—A	12.45	
		D	13.05	
63 25	Pickburn	—	13.15	
69 74	Lawfield Jnc.	—	13.30	
71 53	Mexborough—	—A	13.33	
		D	13.35	
77 26	Rotherham Central	—	13.46	
81 51	Attercliffe Jnc.	—	13.54	
82 39	Darnall —	—A	13.58	
		D	14.00	
85 73	Woodhouse E. Jnc.		14.07	
88 03	Waleswood Jnc.	—	14.10	
93 74	Shireoaks —	—A	14.21	
		D	14.31	
94 69	Brantcliffe E. Jnc.—		14.34	
98 07	Dunnington Col. Jnc.	—	14.42	
105 66	Firbeck A Jnc.	—	15.04	
106 76	Tickhill —	—	15.07	
109 53	St. Catherines Jnc.	—	15.16	
110 28	Black Carr W.	—A	15.21	
		D	15.31	
112 43	Yorkshire Main	—	15.39	
130 51	Crofton South	—	16.10	
131 18	Crofton West	—	16.12	
133 53	Turners Lane	—	16.15	
		D	16.22	
136 15	Normanton	—A	16.28	
		D	16.30	
139 59	Castleford —	—	16.39	
141 70	Ledston —	—	16.46	
146 56	Garforth —	—	17.06	
149 45	Cross Gates	—	17.11	
153 78	Leeds City Sth.	—	17.17	

were passed, and a few steam locos were observed at various scrapyards around the Rotherham area.

The tour eventually arrived on the outskirts of Doncaster at St Catherine's Junction, where our '8F' was ready to take over again, 24 minutes late on schedule; however, some brisk running on the Deane Valley Line helped to regain some time. Passing Wakefield shed an 'A1' 'Pacific' was seen, as the train headed for Normanton and on to Castleford; there the Garforth line was joined (used the previous day by the Royal Train), then the Leeds and Selby line was reached for the last leg of the journey to Leeds City, arrival being 35 minutes late. Our 153-mile journey had taken around 8½ hours, giving the passengers plenty of time to observe the South Yorkshire countryside.

The external condition of '8F' 2-8-0 No 48202 was as dismal as the weather. Here the train heads down the hill on the Cleckheaton branch, past Liversedge station which had closed four months earlier on 12 June. There were plans to re-open this line as a tramway from Low Moor, based on a museum to be built on a site opposite where the steam depot used to be, but by 1992 there was little sign of progress, although lengths of track are still in place. *Gavin Morrison*

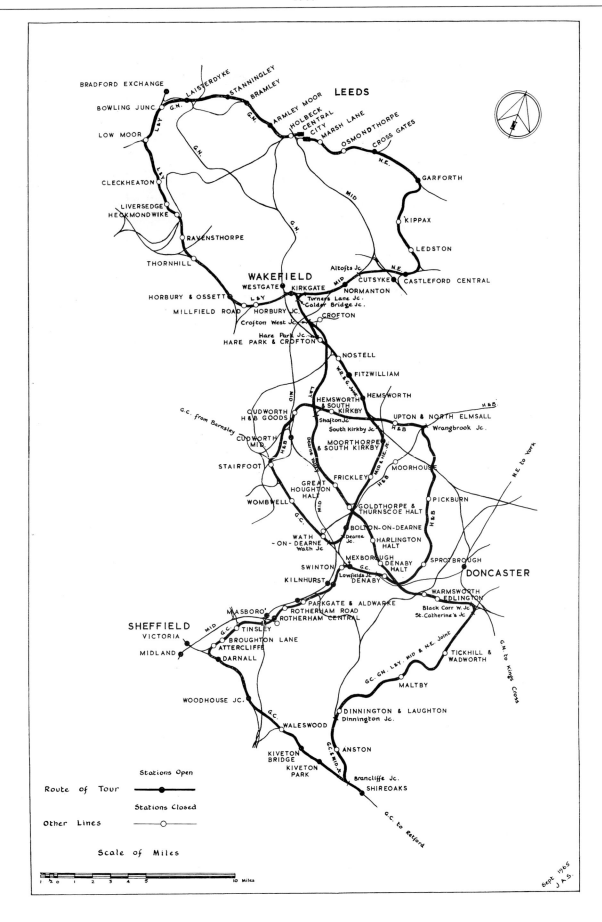

In spite of its external appearance, the locomotive did survive until 1967, when in September of that year steam finished in West Yorkshire. Here the tour is seen later in the day under the wires of the Woodhead route from Wath, passing Mitchells Main signal box on the outskirts of Barnsley. The last train on this electrified line ran on 17 July 1981. *Gavin Morrison*

Sunday 2 January 1966
Somerset and Dorset Rail Tour

The death of the Somerset & Dorset line was a slow and painful process over a few years. The line had always enjoyed a high profile with railway enthusiasts, probably due to the superb photography of the line by the late Ivo Peters. Eventually 3 January 1966 was announced as the day of closure, but difficulties in organising substitute bus services caused the closure to be postponed. The London Branch had got in early and organised this tour, and it was decided to go ahead despite the postponement, especially as the tour was oversubscribed by 120 bookings.

'Merchant Navy' No 35011 *General Steam*

Navigation left Waterloo with 480 passengers on board, Standard '3MT' 2-6-2T No 82019 banking the train out of the terminus. A maximum speed of 82 mph was achieved at Micheldever before water was taken at Southampton. *Queen Mary* was seen in the dry-dock as the special headed towards the New Forest. Bournemouth Central was passed most unusually non-stop through the central road, before Broadstone was reached at 11.30, 5 minutes late.

The first locomotive change of the day took place here; No 35011 came off and was replaced by un-rebuilt 'West Country' No 34015 *Exmouth* and Class

'Merchant Navy' No 35011 *General Steam Navigation* is about to be replaced at Broadstone by 'U' Class 'Mogul' No 31639 and un-rebuilt 'West Country' No 34015 *Exmouth*. Note the undignified posture of a photographer at the bottom of the icy ramp!

No 35011 entered service in December 1944 as No 21C11, and was rebuilt in July 1959. It was eventually withdrawn in February 1966, having covered 1,069,128 miles, and is still in existence as a rusty hulk stored outside Brighton. 'U' Class No 31639 entered service as No A639 in May 1931, and was in the last batch of the class to be withdrawn on 5 June 1966. It was one of only five to receive a general overhaul at Eastleigh as late as June 1963. *Exmouth* entered traffic in November 1945 as No 21C115 and lasted until April 1967, having covered 903,245 miles, when it went to Cashmore's scrapyard at Newport. *Gavin Morrison*

'U' 'Mogul' No 31639. The day had been sunny but frosty, and the platform was extremely icy, so as the photographers rushed from the train to record the change-over, many landed in an undignified heap at the bottom of the platform ramp!

From Broadstone the train made good progress to Evercreech Junction which was reached on time, and where water and photographs were taken again. The stiff climb, mainly at 1 in 50, from Evercreech to the summit at Masbury to cross the Mendips then followed, and the two locomotives gave a good climb,

getting the special to Bath 2 minutes early.

Stanier '8F' No 48309 then took over for a leisurely trip to Mangotsfield, Bristol, Weston-super-Mare and Highbridge, and managed to lose 16 minutes. Ivatt 2-6-2Ts Nos 41307 and 41283 continued for the trip back to Templecombe via Glastonbury, where darkness fell. At Templecombe the 'Merchant Navy' was waiting for the return to Waterloo, where the special arrived 8½ minutes late. More final Somerset & Dorset tours were to follow in the next few weeks.

Above The special approaches Evercreech Junction before tackling the formidable climb, mainly at 1 in 50, to Masbury Summit. The 'Mogul' was a stranger to the Somerset & Dorset line, but the un-rebuilt 'West Country' 'Pacifics' worked over the line for many years, the first revenue-earning trip for one being in May 1951. They were, however, disliked by the Bath crews, mainly due to their enormous appetite for coal and very hot cabs in summer, not to mention their tendency to catch fire, the first occasion being when No 34040 *Crewkerne* went up in flames at Radstock while working the 'Pines Express'. *Gavin Morrison*

Right There was very little opportunity to take an exclusive picture at Evercreech Junction as the locomotives were prepared to tackle the climb to Masbury summit, which they did in fine style. On summer Saturday mornings in years past up to six locomotives could be seen in the centre road siding by the station buildings, waiting to pilot expresses over the Mendips; most would be Midland '2P' 4-4-0s, although in the last years BR Standard '4MT' 75000s were used. *Gavin Morrison*

Sunday 20 March 1966
The Solent Rail Tour

The London branch was responsible for this tour. Originally it was organised to visit both Eastleigh shed and Works, but due to engineering work for the Bournemouth electrification the train had to travel via Salisbury to reach Southampton.

The report in the *Railway Observer* suggested that some participants had difficulty in getting to Waterloo at 9.20 am because of the loss of one hour's sleep due to the clocks being advanced for Summer Time. Others suggested it was more likely due to the branch annual dinner of the previous evening.

The locomotive that had been prepared for the tour was 'West Country' No 34013 *Okehampton*, but it was unable to get to London from Basingstoke in time due to engineering work. Nine Elms therefore hurriedly prepared 'Battle of Britain' No 34089 *602 Squadron*, which after some smart station work was away only 11 minutes late with nine well filled

The two 'USA' tanks used for the trip along the Fawley branch were Nos 30073 and 30064, both in malachite green; their regular duties were as shunters for Eastleigh Works and shed.

Both locomotives were built by Vulcan, having War Department numbers 1959 and 1975 respectively. No 30064 entered service in June 1947 and is credited with having run 301,093 miles before withdrawal in July 1967. It was then stored at Salisbury until being sold in December, going to Droxford and then to Liss under the ownership of the Southern Preservation Company Ltd. It is currently at the Bluebell Railway.

Five examples are preserved, although No 30075 never worked as a British Railways locomotive, having been bought from Yugoslavia. No 30073 did not survive into preservation after withdrawal in December 1966.

The train is approaching Totton where the new flyover was under construction at the time. *Gavin Morrison*

coaches and in the capable hands of Driver Hooper. Standard '4MT' No 80154 provided rear-end assistance out of the terminus.

Where possible good running was made to Basingstoke, and there a crew change to Driver Hoare of Salisbury took place. Our intended locomotive, No 34013, in immaculate condition, was observed on shed at Basingstoke, and the special passed Woking Junction 17 minutes late; in spite of a maximum of 82 mph between Whitchurch and Hurstbourne, other delays caused a 23½ minutes late arrival at Salisbury.

Now with Standard '4MT' No 75070 we headed for Southampton via Romsey to the Ocean Terminal, where we arrived 17 minutes late. Members then toured the old docks, where an added attraction was *Queen Elizabeth*, fresh from a refit, alongside the Ocean Terminal. Some members walked to the docks shed, where D2997 was found. The only steam loco seen in the docks was 'USA' tank No 30069.

Promptly at 13.15 the special departed behind two well-groomed, green-liveried 'USA' tanks, Nos 30064 and 30073, bunker-to-bunker, for what was described in the *Railway Observer* as a slow but noisy trip down the well-used branch to Fawley. The sedate pace on the branch allowed many photographic opportunities, some of which appear here.

No 75070 rejoined the special at Southampton Terminus for the run to Fareham, where it was replaced by 'U' Class 2-6-0 No 31639 for a trip down the Gosport branch, which retained a Victorian atmosphere albeit in a somewhat decayed state.

At Fareham the '4MT' and the 'U' joined forces for the return to Waterloo via the Portsmouth Direct line. In spite of an additional photographic stop at Portchester, the train was only 1 minute late at Guildford. Excellent running continued following the unusual route via Guildford London Road, Effingham Junction and Oxshott, rejoining the main line at Hampton Court Junction. An unscheduled stop at Wimbledon made the train 1 minute late, but more enthusiastic running via East Putney got us back at 19.42.

This was obviously a good day out, which in spite of a difficult start ended in fine style.

The train on its outward journey, crossing the new road to Fawley. Note the little Austin A35 car, whose owner was following the train. *Gavin Morrison*

16 & 30 April 1966   Longmoor

With the imminent closure of the Longmoor Military Railway, the Society ran two tours there. Some 400 members and friends took part on the first day, gathering at Waterloo in preparation for the run to Woking hauled by Class 'U' 2-6-0 No 31639 and Class 'N' 2-6-0 No 31411. These two once numerous classes could only muster five representatives between them on the tour date.

A beautifully clean 'WD' 2-10-0 No 600 *Gordon* hauled the train to Liss, then LMR 'WD' 0-6-0ST No 195 joined No 600 to haul the train to Longmoor Down station. On arrival the tour party divided, one half visiting the depot and the other riding behind 'WD' 0-6-0ST No 196 to tour the line around the Hollywater loop. The highlight of the latter trip was photographic 'run-pasts', only spoiled by the appalling weather conditions.

Gordon worked the return journey from Bordon to Staines, where BR 2-6-0 No 77014, recently arrived from the NER to the SR, hauled the train to

Windsor & Eton Riverside. From there the two 'Moguls' worked the final leg of the tour to Waterloo via Staines and Brentford.

Because of the enormous demand, a second tour was run two weeks later, this time in glorious sunny conditions. No 31411, which had been withdrawn, was replaced by No 31791 which joined No 31639 following the same route as the first tour. *Gordon* again performed in sparkling fashion on both legs of the tour. Unfortunately No 77014 was unfit to work the train, so Standard Class '5' 4-6-0 No 73114 *Etarre* was used, following the same route as on the previous week, with the 'Moguls' making the final run to Waterloo.

The two tours were a great tribute to the staff on the Longmoor Military Railway, who spared no effort to make both days a great success, and the SR who provided the wide range of motive power and well-stocked buffet cars, which on both occasions were 'dry' by the time Waterloo was reached!

This was very much a swan song for 'N' Class 'Mogul' No 31411, seen in this picture at Windsor & Eton Riverside with 'U' Class No 31639. It had already been withdrawn and was reinstated for the occasion, but was not available two weeks later for the second tour. *Gavin Morrison*

In spite of the terrible weather conditions, 'WD' 2-10-0 No 600 *Gordon* still looked superb in its blue livery, and is seen here at the head of the RCTS train at Longmoor. Happily the locomotive is now preserved at the Severn Valley Railway. *Gavin Morrison*

'WD' 0-6-0ST No 196 has great difficulty in getting started in the appalling weather conditions on one of the 'run-pasts' on the Longmoor system during the first tour. *Rodney Lissenden*

In stark contrast, the second tour two weeks later ran in glorious weather. Here *Gordon* sparkles in the sun as it approaches Haslemere *en route* for Liss and its own railway. *Rodney Lissenden*

Sunday 19 March 1967
The Lancastrian Rail Tour

The Society Annual General Meeting had been held in Manchester on Saturday 18 March and, as had become the tradition, the host branch, Lancashire and North West, had organised this tour for the Sunday. Departure was from Manchester Victoria, and at the head of the seven coaches was Stockport's only working 'Britannia', No 70015 *Apollo*. In spite of only having another five months to go before withdrawal, the locomotive had been repainted in unlined green livery by the enthusiastic shed staff at Edgeley. The route was a comprehensive tour of Lancashire not designed for high-speed running, although the Newton Heath crew gave the passengers some

'Britannia' No 70015 *Apollo* was built in June 1951, and initially allocated to Camden shed, before being transferred to Stratford in December of that year. The locomotive is, however, normally associated with the Western Region, where it was transferred in September 1953, allocated to Old Oak Common. It remained on the Western until the diesels took over main-line diagrams, and was then transferred to the London Midland Region at Stockport, along with two other members of the class, No 70004 *William Shakespeare* and No 70026 *Polar Star*. *Apollo* was to survive until August 1967, only five months after the tour.

Apollo's nameplates and numberplate were replicas - even the RCTS headboard was not the usual small stainless steel one. The locomotive is seen at Rose Grove before running down the branch to Padiham. *Gavin Morrison*

exhilarating climbs up the various banks.

The special headed first for Bolton, then the triangle at Burriden Junction, just south of the station, was taken, thence to Castleton via Bury Knowsley over a section of line soon to be re-opened by the East Lancashire Railway group.

The main line was taken to Todmorden through the famous 2,885-yard Summit Tunnel.

The now long-removed side of the triangle to Stansfield Hall Junction was traversed prior to the formidable climb to Copy Pit at 1 in 60. The driver opened up the 'Britannia', which responded well, with the exhaust echo bouncing off the sides of the narrow valley and giving a speed of 36 mph at Cornholme, half-way up the hill. Arrival at Rose Grove West was early, but a delay of $11^{1}/_{2}$ minutes occurred to allow the Inspector time to walk from Gannow Junction to join us; somehow the train had failed to pick him up, so no doubt he had something to say as he climbed on board.

After his arrival *Apollo* headed down the Padiham branch which served the power station, and still does in 1992. On the return journey the special departed 8 minutes early and made a spirited ascent of the 1 in 40 bank back up to Rose Grove, as can be seen in the accompanying photograph. The locomotive then visited the shed for water and coal.

At 12.30, 2 minutes late, the train departed and headed west to Blackburn and on to Feniscowles where *Apollo* ran round the train and returned to Cherry Tree Junction. Propelling was necessary before the train could cross over to return to Blackburn, where another reversal was necessary.

The next destination of the special was Bolton, which involved the steep climb to Waltons Sidings at 1 in 64/75. Having passed the summit at 31 mph, 60 mph was achieved down the other side, and arrival at Bolton West Junction was 5 minutes early.

The special arrives at Padiham with the locomotive blowing off. *Gavin Morrison*

At Padiham the locomotive reversed, and a spirited climb of the 1 in 40 to Rose Grove followed. *Gavin Morrison*

Again the special headed west to Lostock Junction and on to Hindley. The Whalley line was taken at De Trafford Junction, but several delays occurred in this area, giving the keen crew an incentive for a fast trip down the West Coast Main Line, 82 mph being achieved before Farrington Junction. The diverted 'Royal Scot' caused the train further delays, and there was a crew change at Farrington, where Lostock Hall driver Norris and fireman Charnley joined the footplate. The locomotive also made another shed visit for water. Eventually, 12 minutes late, the train set off across the West Lancashire plain to Burscough North Junction, where a Liverpool Division Inspector joined the crew.

Onward towards Southport via Meols Cop and St Lukes, the train took the avoiding line on to the electrified line to Liverpool. An attempt to gain time was made with 64 mph at Freshfield before a preceding electric was caught up; this curbed the crew's enthusiasm, but in spite of everything the special arrived at Hall Road on time.

At Bootle Junction the train took the LNWR Alexandra Dock line through 'Bomb Alley', so named locally thanks to the activities of the local hooligans, followed by a leisurely run across Liverpool. Eventually Olive Mount Junction was passed 11 minutes late, and hopes were high for a fast run to Manchester, but this was not to be - due to checks Ordsall Lane was passed 15 minutes late, but an unchecked run via Deansgate and Oxford Road brought the special to Manchester Piccadilly only 9^1/$_2$ minutes late.

Saturday 6 May 1967
North Eastern No 3 Rail Tour

This was another West Riding branch tour and, by comparison with many that the branch had run, was one of the more straightforward. It started at Bradford Exchange, which even in the best of weather conditions had a rather gloomy atmosphere about it, but in the pouring rain with low cloud was enough to cause the photographers plenty of problems. As it turned out, a really atmospheric picture was recorded.

A long time resident of Holbeck depot, and one of the last 'Jubilees' in service, No 45562 *Alberta* was our locomotive, in fine external condition. Our Inspector on the footplate was as usual Geoff Wilson, who always did his best to give us a good trip.

A 9.18 am, on time, *Alberta* left and made a splendid noise on the 1 in 50 climb to Bowling Junction and on to Low Moor, before taking the Spen Valley line to Healey Mills. It is interesting to note that a slack had to be made for the earthworks for the M1 extension at Horbury Junction. Water was taken at Wakefield Westgate, where additional passengers joined the train, then we set off past the Motive Power Depot, which was due for early closure. At Crotton West Junction we took the line to Featherstone, which had lost its passenger service in January (but happily in 1991 got it back). Good progress was made to York where the train took the goods-only lines to York North yard.

The loco crews changed here, and it was not long before *Alberta* was heading down the East Coast Main Line, with a maximum of 72 mph before Raskelf. At Northallerton there was a brief stop to remove a non-fare-paying passenger, and for a genuine ticker-holder to join. The special then continued to Croft, where a 'Deltic'-hauled King's Cross express passed on the up before we could take the Geneva Curve to allow us to join the Stockton & Darlington line at Oak Tree Junction on the way to Middlesbrough, passing Thornaby depot *en route*.

At Middlesbrough *Alberta* left the train for West Hartlepool depot for servicing, and was replaced by English Electric Type 3 No D6778, later to become No 37078, which is still giving main-line service in 1992.

The diesel then took the tour to Redcar and up the 1 in 70 bank to Skinningrove. A quick reversal and departure was made to try and placate the signalman at Saltburn West Junction who had expressed his displeasure at having his normal Saturday activities interrupted by the tour.

We arrived back at Middlesbrough for the second time, then departed for Whitby. In spite of torrential rain at Grosmont, the weather at Whitby was reasonable, the journey having been uneventful except for overtaking a point-to-point event *en route*.

In 1967 there was little of railway interest left at Whitby, so the passengers had a walk into the town. On time, at 16.43, the Class 37 set off back to Middlesbrough, where *Alberta* took over, leaving 2 minutes early. Not far from the station a local vandal celebrated the passing of the train by throwing a stone which cracked the glass on the loco spectacle.

Although booked on the up slow from Northallerton, the train headed on the up fast, but suffered a succession of double yellows virtually all the way to York.

Water was taken at York, then after some agitation from the branch chairman the train got the 'right away'. A block failure around Church Fenton lost 6 minutes, but time was gained to Wakefield Kirkgate.

The last leg of the journey involved the climb of the 1 in 44 Greetland bank, and *Alberta* made a splendid ascent, raising the echoes up the Calder Valley. I was fortunate enough to be travelling on the footplate, and as we passed the bottom of my garden at Lightcliffe three blasts on the whistle were given to inform my wife I would be back in time for a meal!

Unlike some of the branch tours, we arrived back 11 minutes early at 21.26.

Bradford Exchange was a depressing station even in ideal weather conditions, but on a wet misty morning it presented a sorry sight. In sharp contrast to the gloom of the station, however, superb Holbeck 'Jubilee' No 45562 *Alberta*, well shrouded in its own steam, waits to do battle with the 1 in 50 gradient to Bowling Junction.
Built in August 1934 by the North British Locomotive Co, *Alberta* survived until the end of steam in the West Riding of Yorkshire in September 1967. It is recorded as being allocated to Holbeck in 1945, so it spent at least 22 years at the depot. It is of interest that out of the 22 'Jubilees' allocated to 20A in 1945, 12 of them were still allocated to the depot upon withdrawal in the mid-1960s. *Gavin Morrison*

R.C.T.S., WEST RIDING BRANCH.
NORTH EASTERN NO. 3 RAILTOUR

1Z06 09.18 BRADFORD (EXCHANGE) - WHITBY 6.5.67

–	Bradford Exchange	D.	09.18	–	Whitby	D	16.43
2.76	Low Moor		09/25	183.43	Grosmont		16/59
5.56	Cleckheaton		09/??	186.51	Glaisdale		17/07
7.51	Heckmondwike		09/35	193.63	Castleton Moor	A	17.20
10.13	Thornhill Jct.		09/40			D	17.24
			SL	201.18	Battersby	A	17.39
11.22	Midland Junction		09/45			D	17.49
14.67	Horbury Junction		09/49	207.55	Nunthorpe		18/01
17.10	Wakefield Kirkgate	A	09.53	212.23	Middlesbrough	A	18.13
		D.	09.59			D	18.19
18.68	Crofton West		10/03	218.40	Eaglescliffe		18/31
23.08	Featherstone		10/11	233.13	Northallerton	A	18.51
25.61	Pontefract East		10/16			D	18.52
27.41	Ferrybridge		10/21	240.73	Thirsk		19/05
30.05	Burton Salmon		10/26	253.30	Tollerton		19/25
36.00	Church Fenton		10/33	263.09	York	A	19.38
47.25	York Yard South		10/47			D	19.41
47.41	York Yard North		10/57	273.68	Church Fenton		19/56
68.54	Thirsk		11/22½	279.63	Burton Salmon		20/04
76.34	Northallerton	A	11.31	284.04	Castleford (Central)		20/11
		D	11.32	286.59	Altofts Junction		20/18
89.61	Croft Ground Frame	A	11.50	287.48	Normanton		20/20
		D	12.00	290.55	Wakefield Kirkgate	A	20.27
90.28	Geneva Sig. Box		12/05			D	20.42
98.24	Eaglescliffe		12/18	292.78	Horbury Junction		20/47
104.41	Middlesbrough	A	12.28	296.43	Midland Junction		20/52
		D	12.34	300.04	Mirfield		20/58
112.25	Redcar Central		12/46	304.10	Brighouse		21/05
116.49	Saltburn West Junction		12/56	307.38	Greetland		21/13
123.28	Crag Hall	A	13.12	308.52	Dryclough Junction		21/17
		D	13.23	309.39	Halifax	A	21.20
130.07	Saltburn West Junction		13/40			D	21.24
134.31	Redcar Central		13/48	314.55	Low Moor		21/31
142.15	Middlesbrough	A	14.00	317.51	Bradford (Exchange)	A	21.37
		D	14.07				
146.63	Nunthorpe		14/21				
153.20	Battersby	A	14.33				
		D	14.41				
160.55	Castleton Moor		14/57				
167.67	Glaisdale		15/11				
170.75	Grosmont		15/17				
177.19	Whitby	A	15.36				

From Middlesbrough the train was hauled by English Electric Type 3 No D6778. On the return journey from Whitby to Middlesbrough a photographic stop was made at Castleton Moor, where the special was passed by a Middlesbrough-Whitby service train formed of a Class '101' DMU. The Castleton to Grosmont section of the line was opened in October 1865. *Gavin Morrison*

Whitby station dated from 1847, and until 1953 had an overall roof. There was also a locomotive depot in the town, which closed in April 1959. No D6778 waits at the head of the train ready for the return journey on the Esk Valley Line to Middlesbrough. Twenty-five years later the locomotive is still active as No 37078, a Metals Sector locomotive based at Cardiff. *Gavin Morrison*

'Jubilees' were not very common in the Middlesbrough area. *Alberta* is seen ready to depart on the return trip to Bradford. Note the highly polished buffers. *Gavin Morrison*

18 June 1967
Farewell to Southern Steam

A sense of sadness was felt by many members and friends on this tour, which was to be the last of so many enjoyable steam-hauled railtours on the South Western Division of the Southern Region.

The 12-coach train left Waterloo double-headed by BR Standard Class '5' 4-6-0 No 73029 and 'West Country' 4-6-2 No 34023 *Blackmore Vale*; the pair worked to Fareham via East Putney, the new Guildford line, Effingham Junction and Portsmouth.

'Battle of Britain' No 34089 *602 Squadron* then worked the train from Fareham to Southampton, where 'West Country' No 34108 *Wincanton* was attached for the run to Bournemouth and Wareham. On arrival BR Class '4' 2-6-4T No 80146 was attached to the rear of the train, and together with No 34089 worked to Swanage and back. *602 Squadron* then took the train single-handed to Weymouth, *Wincanton* having run light to Bournemouth MPD.

The return journey to Waterloo was hauled by Nos 34023 and 34089 to Salisbury, then 'Merchant Navy' No 35013 *Blue Funnel* worked the final leg to Waterloo, attaining 85 mph at Red Post Junction - a fitting farewell to SR steam.

Steam on the Southern finally came to an end on 9 July 1967, and with it some extremely exciting running, speeds of around 100 mph having been reported by enthusiasts on the Bournemouth workings.

A good selection of locomotives were used for the tour, representing most of the classes that remained, and for the first leg the 12-coach train was entrusted to BR Standard '5MT' No 73029 in green livery together with un-rebuilt 'West Country' Pacific No 34023 *Blackmore Vale*. This picture shows the train south of Petersfield.

Blackmore Vale is now preserved on the Bluebell Railway, having travelled 921,268 miles in its 21 years of service; it is interesting to think that it has now spent 26 years in preservation. *Rodney Lissenden*

Well cleaned for the occasion, Standard '4MT' 2-6-4T No 80146 was used for the journey along the Swanage branch, with rebuilt 'Battle of Britain' No 34089 *602 Squadron* at the other end. This photograph shows the special returning from Swanage. *Rodney Lissenden*

No 34089 *602 Squadron* hauled the special to Weymouth where, for the return journey to Salisbury, it was piloted by *Blackmore Vale*. The pair are shown tackling the climb out of Weymouth past Upwey to the summit at Dorchester.
No 34089 was built in December 1948, then rebuilt in November 1960. It travelled a total of 661,252 miles, of which 402,834 were before rebuilding. Only one rebuilt locomotive, No 34001 *Exeter*, managed to exceed 1 million miles, with a total of 1,079,987. Two un-rebuilt examples exceeded the figure, with No 34006 *Bude* achieving the highest of them all with 1,099,338
Rodney Lissenden

Sunday 16 July 1967
A4 to Glasgow Rail Tour

The organisation of this tour by the West Riding branch proved a nightmare due to all the engineering works that were taking place on the main lines, which had always been a good reason for not running such tours on Sunday.

With 490 passengers on board, the special got off to a 9½ minutes late start due to the buffet car crew getting stuck in a lift with all the refreshments! Our locomotive was of particular interest, as it was 'A4' No 60019 *Bittern*, which was by then privately owned by Mr G. S. Drury, and kept at York. The locomotive had been purchased one week after withdrawal from Ferryhill depot at Aberdeen in September 1966, and was apparently still in good order.

The tour could have been advertised as 'travel wrong line to Glasgow from Leeds', such were the number of engineering possessions encountered! The first of these occurred after only 12 miles of the 453-mile trip had been completed, at Hirst Wood, but with an enthusiastic Holbeck crew, driver Blakey in charge, we were only 12 minutes late at Skipton. Water was taken there instead of at the booked stop at Hellifield, and we were fortunate that the line was clear for the climb from Settle Junction to Blea Moor. The Society already held the record with steam for the climb with *City of Liverpool* on 9 July 1961, but the 'A4' put up a superb performance, passing Blea Moor box at 52 mph. By that point the 18 minutes late departure from Skipton had been reduced to only 4 minutes, and lively running to Carlisle resulted in a 1 minute early arrival, much to the relief of the organising committee.

Kingmoor men then took over for the next leg, but it was once more 'wrong line' working from Kingmoor to Gretna, and, as the pilotman was on the up 'Thames Clyde' express, a 26-minute delay occurred. The timings had allowed a 22-minute wait at Beattock Station to gain the wrong line to Greskine, so water was taken before backing across to the up line and taking a Type 1 (Class '20') as banker.

The banker got left behind at the first attempt to depart, but all was well at the second. In spite of everything the summit was passed 3 minutes early,

and it was then plain sailing to Craigenhill for the next 'wrong line' working to Carluke. It was with great relief and surprise to all that we arrived at Glasgow Central 8 minutes ahead of schedule.

Visits to Eastfield and Polmadie depots had been organised, as well as to the Glasgow Transport Museum. Departure from Glasgow Central was at 17.39, the route taken being via Paisley Gilmoor Street to Dalry Junction, to join the direct line to Kilmarnock and regain the Glasgow & South Western main line south. Good progress was made, and from passing Kilmarnock 11½ minutes late, the deficit had been reduced to 1 minute by Annan. I can personally vouch for this good progress as I was following the train by car to get photographs, and in spite of a virtually empty road I never managed to get far enough in front of the 'A4' until Gretna, having taken the last picture at Hurlford.

A 13-minute delay occurred at Gretna awaiting a pilotman, who gave us permission to proceed but did not actually travel on the footplate. The tour was doing very well under the circumstances to be only 23 minutes late at Carlisle, where the passengers were delighted to see driver Blakey and his fireman awaiting us to take us back over the Settle and Carlisle line. We were promised we would be treated to some lively running.

The special was going in fine style, in excess of 80 mph at Lazonby, when we drew to an unscheduled stop at Culgaith. Thoughts of an engine failure drew mild panic from the organising committee, as visions of stranded passengers at Leeds on a Sunday night loomed up in their minds - after all, it was already 21.20. However, inquiries revealed that a loud bang had been heard by the crew from what they believed was the locomotive, so they had stopped to examine as a precaution. From then on the running became more sedate and the speed restrained, but Skipton was reached at 22.36, only 18 minutes down. In fact, in spite of everything there had been a gain of 7 minutes on the schedule from Carlisle. Eventually, much to the relief of the committee, our arrival at Leeds was 23.16, only 25 minutes late. In spite of all the headaches, the West Riding branch had once gain successfully completed another major tour.

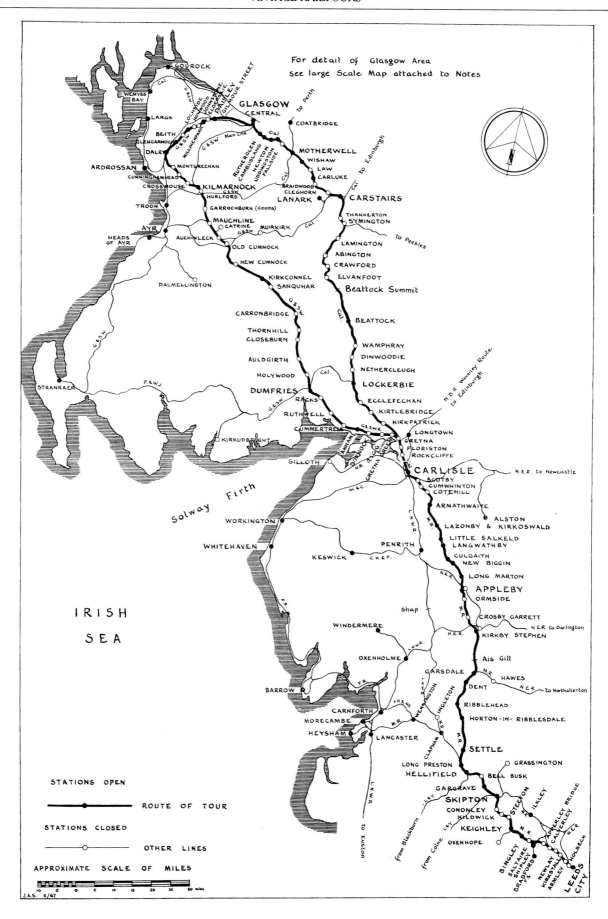

For detail of Glasgow Area
see large Scale Map attached to Notes

STATIONS OPEN

━━━━━●━━━━━   ROUTE OF TOUR

STATIONS CLOSED

──────○──────   OTHER LINES

APPROXIMATE SCALE OF MILES

J.A.S. 5/67

Bittern blows off as it crosses the River Eden at Carlisle and approaches Etterby Junction near Kingmoor depot. It is running on the slow lines prior to crossing over to the down main.

The locomotive was fitted with the double chimney in September 1957. It is always associated with Heaton and Gateshead depots, where it was allocated between December 1937 and October 1963, before being sent to Scotland for its last three years. *Gavin Morrison*

Outward			
M. Ch.			
0.00	Leeds City	... dep.	09.40
10.56	Shipley Leeds Jct. ...		09.56
16.79	Keighley	...	10.16
25.00	Snaygill	...	10.24
26.14	Skipton	... arr.	10.26
		dep.	10.28
36.15	Hellifield	... arr.	10.42W
		dep.	10.48W
39.35	Settle Jct.	...	10.52
53.35	Blea Moor	...	11.14
64.50	Ais Gill	...	11.27
82.15	Appleby West	...	11.44
112.08	Petteril Bridge Jct.		12.15
113.00	Carlisle	... arr.	12.17W
		dep.	12.27W
113.59	Carlisle No. 3	...	12.29
			GL
121.48	Gretna Jct.	...	12.54
138.53	Lockerbie	...	13.14
152.48	Beattock	... arr.	13.29
		dep.	13.51
—	Greskine	... arr.	14.15
		dep.	14.17
162.49	Beattock Summit ...		14.36
179.65	Symington	...	14.55
186.38	Carstairs	...	15.02
188.58	Lanark Jct.	...	15.05
—	Craigenhill	... arr.	15.09
		dep.	15.17
197.01	Law Jct.	...	15.31
202.32	Motherwell	...	15.39
206.63	Uddingston	...	15.44
208.51	Newton	...	15.47
212.09	Rutherglen	...	15.50
214.21	Eglington St.	...	15.54
215.21	Glasgow (Cen.)	... arr.	15.57

Return			
M. Ch.			
0.00	Glasgow Central	... dep.	17.32
1.51	Shields Jct.	...	17.36
6.16	Arkleston Jct.	...	17.41
7.24	Paisley Gilmour St.		17.43
9.24	Elderslie	...	17.46
16.08	Lochside	...	17.53
23.07	Dalry Jct.	...	18.01
33.27	Kilmarnock	...	18.17
42.59	Mauchline	...	18.33
54.40	New Cumnock	...	18.48
65.23	Sanquhar	...	19.00
77.18	Thornhill	...	19.12
91.33	Dumfries	...	19.26
106.70	Annan	...	19.44
115.60	Gretna Jct.	...	19.55
			GL
123.49	Carlisle No. 3	...	20.15
124.28	Carlisle	... arr.	20.17W
		dep.	20.25W
125.20	Petterill Bridge Jct.		20.27
155.13	Appleby West	...	21.06
172.58	Ais Gill	...	21.34
183.73	Blea Moor	...	21.46
197.73	Settle Jct.	...	21.59
201.13	Hellifield	... arr.	22.02W
		dep.	22.07W
211.14	Skipton	... arr.	22.18
		dep.	22.20
212.28	Snaygill	...	22.22
220.29	Keighley	...	22.30
226.52	Shipley Leeds Jct.		22.37
237.28	Leeds City	... arr.	22.52

Right Half-way up Beattock bank at Greskine, the Kingmoor driver awaits the signal from the guard to head off 'wrong line' towards the summit. Note that *Bittern* was running with a 50A shedplate, and with York painted on the front, although 'A4s' were never actually allocated to the depot. *Gavin Morrison*

Below The special negotiates another 'wrong line' working, as it reverses across from the down to the up line at Craigenhill, the summit between Carstairs and Motherwell. *Gavin Morrison*

Bittern is going very well on the 7-mile climb at 1 in 100/90 from Hurlford to Garrochburn on the Glasgow & South Western main line. Gavin Morrison

Sunday 16 June 1968   Dalesman No 2

This was the West Riding branch's farewell to steam on British Rail. In fact, by this time steam was only available on Midland Region lines, so the tour started from Leeds at 10.02 am headed by Type 2 D7568, later to become Class '25' No 25218. This was the last branch tour hauled by BR steam, and several of the 380 passengers aboard, including myself, had also been travelling on the first West Riding steam tour back in 1957.

The special only got as far as Wortley Junction

Sulzer Type 2 No D7568, later to become Class '25' No 25218, approaches Halifax from the 1,105-yard Beacon Hill Tunnel. The station was originally owned by the Lancashire & Yorkshire Railway, but the Great Northern also had tracks into it which resulted in fierce rivalry. The line to one of the town's other stations on the GN route, at North Bridge, can be seen curving away to the left. Passenger traffic over it had ceased in 1954 but it had remained open for freight to Holmfield and Pellon until 1960.
Gavin Morrison

before being stopped, as the signalman did not realise that the train was going to Carnforth via the Calder Valley, and not down the Midland line. Progress to Stansfield Hall was unremarkable, but here 'Britannia' No 70013 *Oliver Cromwell* was waiting to take over the nine-coach train.

It was my good fortune to travel on the footplate of the 'Britannia', and what most of the passengers didn't know was the driver was in fact an RCTS member of the North West branch, and had got the job via some imaginative rostering.

Needless to say, we were treated to a good climb up the 1 in 78 to Copy Pit, speed rising to 30 mph. This gave the lineside photographers and sound recordists plenty to be pleased about, as well as the hundreds of casual spectators by the roadside.

A rapid if somewhat uncomfortable ride then followed to Gannow Junction and on to Accrington, where we came to a stand. There followed rapid acceleration onwards towards Blackburn, and then to Preston, a 76 mph maximum being achieved. Water was taken at Preston, and a crew change was made; Carnforth men took over and did the best they could in spite of several signal and permanent way checks to Carnforth.

Carnforth depot presented a sad sight, housing withdrawn locos and the last few still in service. Of particular interest were the locomotives destined for preservation, namely 'B1' No 61306, 2-6-4Ts Nos 42073 and 42085, and Ivatt 2-6-0 No 46441.

The tour then continued with *Oliver Cromwell* taking us over the Midland line to Skipton, with a photographic stop at Clapham. Here we said goodbye to BR steam for the last time and Class '24' No D5113 took over the train for a trip up the Grassington branch.

After reversing with some difficulty, the journey back to Skipton was made, and then to Keighley, where buses were organised to take passengers to Haworth to see the Keighley & Worth Valley engines in the yard. Little Barclay saddle tank No 2226 was in steam, and Worth Valley No 72 (the 'USA' tank) and Ivatt No 41241 were also on view, already painted for the preserved line's opening on 29 June.

It was 20.00 before the train left Keighley for Shipley Junction and an evening trip to Guiseley and Ilkley. An 18 minutes late departure was reduced to 13 by the time the Class '24' rolled into Leeds City, and so ended the West Riding branch's last tour using BR steam.

SCHEDULE

M. Ch.					M. Ch.			
0.00	Leeds City	...	dep.	10.00	97.70	Wennington	... pass	14.16
0.49	Whitehall Jct.	...	pass	10.03	105.28	Clapham	... arr.	14.28
0.68	Holbeck Jct.	...	pass	10.04			dep.	14.43
7.48	Laisterdyke	...	pass	10.16	112.66	Settle Jct.	... pass	14.55
9.39	Bowling Jct.	...	pass	10.21	116.06	Hellifield	... pass	14.59
11.14	Low Moor	...	pass	10.25	126.07	Skipton Stn. N.	... arr.	15L13
16.30	Halifax	...	arr.	10.32			dep.	15L23
			dep.	10.34	128.01	Embsay Jct.	... pass	15.29
20.02	Sowerby Bridge	...	pass	10.40	136.39	Grassington	... arr.	16.00
25.02	Hebden Bridge	...	pass	10.46			dep.	17.00
29.01	Hall Royd Jct.	...	pass	10.50	144.77	Embsay Jct.	... pass	17.29
29.21	Stansfield Hall	...	arr.	10L52	146.71	Skipton N. Jct.	... arr.	17L35
			dep.	11L02			dep.	17L45
33.26	Copy Pit	...	pass	11.11	148.05	Snaygill	... pass	17.47
39.14	Rose Grove	...	pass	11.21	156.06	Keighley	... arr.	17.57
43.61	Accrington	...	pass	11.31			dep.	20.00
49.00	Blackburn	...	pass	11.41	162.29	Shipley/Leeds Jct.	... pass	20.09
58.02	Lostock Hall Jct.	...	pass	11.54	162.47	Shipley/Guiseley Jct.	... pass	20.10
59.39	Farington Curve Jct.	...	pass	11.59	166.72	Guiseley	... pass	20.19
61.04	Preston N.U.	...	pass	12.07	172.72	Ilkley	... arr.	20.29
70.42	Garstang & C.	...	pass	12.20			dep.	20.45
82.03	Lancaster	...	pass	12.33	182.11	Apperley Jct.	... pass	21.00
88.22	Carnforth	...	arr.	12.40	188.08	Wortley Jct.	... pass	21.10
			dep.	14.00	189.03	Leeds City	... arr.	21.13
88.46	Carnforth E. Jct.	...	pass	14.01				

L — Engine change

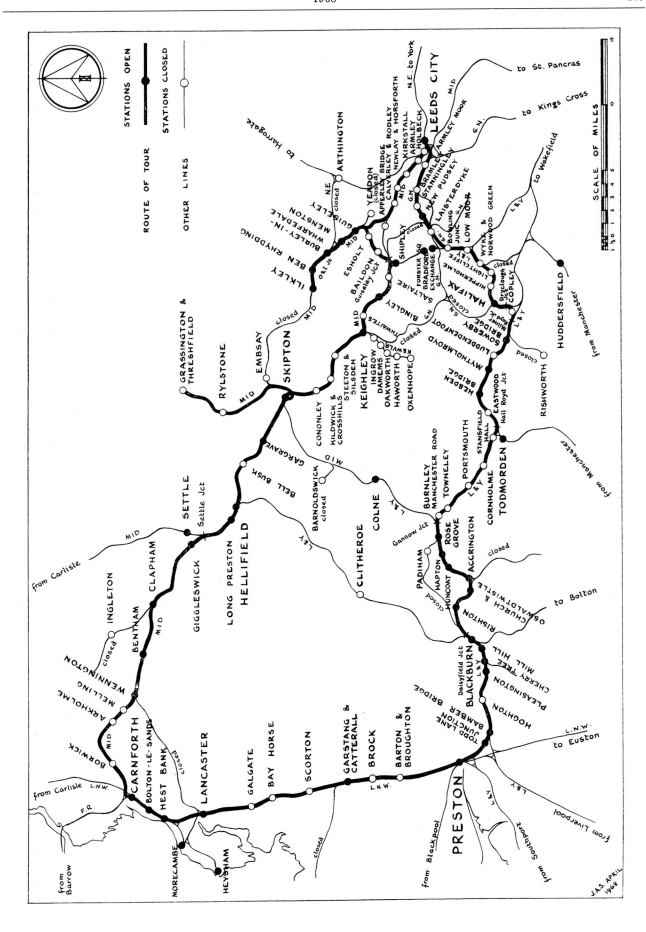

The road ahead is clear for the driver of 'Britannia' No 70013 *Oliver Cromwell* as the special prepares to leave Accrington *en route* to Preston and Carnforth. *Gavin Morrison*

Oliver Cromwell makes a fine sight as it tackles the short grade out of Hellifield on its way to Skipton, before a Class '24' diesel took over for the rest of the tour. No 70013 worked the last British Railways steam special north over the Settle and Carlisle line on the famous '15-guinea special' on 11 August 1968, before returning light engine to Bressingham in Norfolk for preservation. *Gavin Morrison*

The Grassington branch lost its passenger service on 21 September 1930, but the top section of the line from Swinden limeworks to Grassington did not finally close until 9 August 1969; the rest of the branch is still in use today for the Tilcon lime trains, now hauled by Class '60' diesels. The Dalesman No 2 tour must have been one of, if not the, last passenger train to visit Grassington. The photograph shows the terminus station buildings, and the Station Master directing operations as the special makes a cautious approach. As 37 minutes had been allowed in the schedule for the 10-mile journey up the branch, there was no need to hurry.

The locomotive is Type 2 No D5113, later to become Class '24' No 24113, the last of the class to be built without the roof-mounted indicator panels. It was constructed at Darlington in January 1961, but only lasted until December 1976, being scrapped at BREL Doncaster. *Gavin Morrison*

The scene from this bridge today is very different. The main road now passes to the right of the picture, and a complex of sidings has been installed on either side of where the train is shown. The quarry is still very active and presents an unpleasant blot on the landscape, but at least it still provides some business for British Rail. *Gavin Morrison*

Sunday 5 January 1969
Farewell to the Waverley Route

The West Riding branch was lucky to get a 'Deltic' for the tour, as back in 1969 they were very heavily diagrammed and not usually available for railtours. Be that as it may, it was an immaculate blue-liveried D9007 *Pinza* that departed from Leeds City at 9.43 am, 13 minutes behind schedule.

Due to several delays *en route*, the 'Deltic' was given plenty of opportunity to show its capabilities, and it was the hill-climbing which really produced plenty of excitement, although some of the speeds at which the curves were taken were not appreciated by the restaurant car crew!

Skipton was reached at 10.15 am with a maximum of 82 mph near Cononley. After Skipton rapid progress was made, with 77 mph just after Bell Busk, and all was going well until we were brought to a dead stand by the signalwoman at Settle to inform the crew of some permanent way work.

This check gave the crew the opportunity to show what a 'Deltic' could do on the climb to Blea Moor; without it the train would have sailed up the climb without effort. By Helwith Bridge speed was over 60 mph and continued to rise until the summit was passed at just under 70 mph, which made our previous exploits with *City of Liverpool* and *Bittern* look

THE RAILWAY CORRESPONDENCE
AND TRAVEL SOCIETY

ITINERARY OF THE

*Farewell to the Waverley
Route Tour*

LEEDS CITY — SKIPTON — AIS GILL — CARLISLE
RICCARTON JUNCTION — HAWICK — FOUNTAINHALL
EDINBURGH WAVERLEY

SUNDAY, 5th JANUARY, 1969

A light covering of snow is present at probably the most remote station on the BR network in 1969, Riccarton. This was formerly Riccarton Junction when there was a branch to Hexham, which lost its passenger service on 15 October 1956. For many years there was no road access to this lonely station, but courtesy of the Forestry Commission one was available during the last years of the line's operation. There was also a small shed here which in latter days housed Standard BR 2-6-0s, Ivatt 2-6-0s and an ex-North British 'J36' for working the branch and banking.

No D9007 *Pinza* makes a fine sight in the winter sunshine during a photographic stop. *Gavin Morrison*

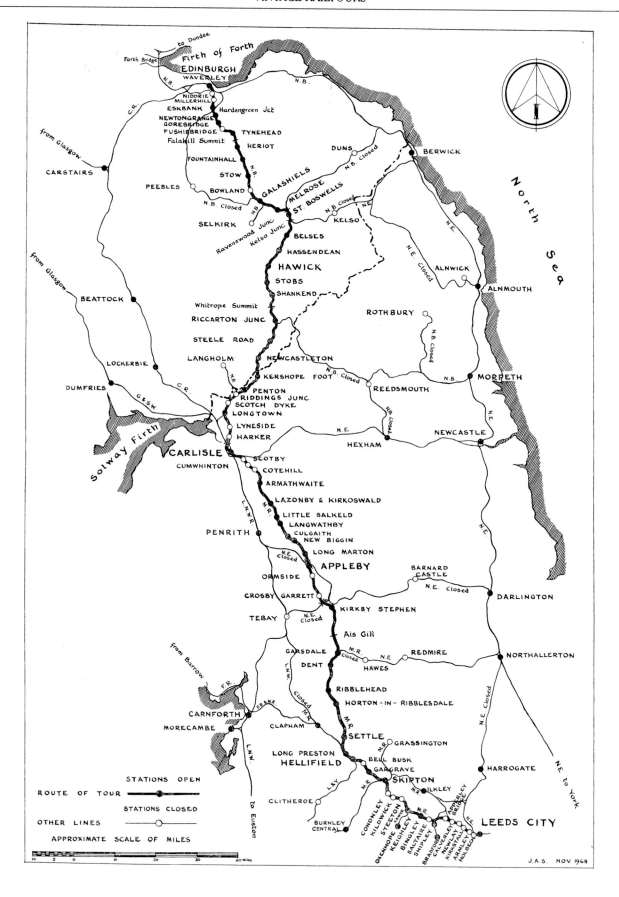

J.A.S. NOV 1968

rather slow. We saw the Settle and Carlisle line at its best, in a variety of weather ranging from a blizzard to brilliant sun. In spite of everything the train was only 5½ minutes late at Carlisle, having attained a maximum of 92 mph near Little Salkeld.

The train was soon heading north to Canal Junction, where the Waverley Route was joined. By comparison with the Settle and Carlisle line, steady progress was made to Riccarton Junction, where to the delight of the photographers a stop was made in the sun and snow.

The departure to Whitrope summit had problems, as the track had been smeared with grease on the 1 in 75, but momentum was kept even if it was at less than walking pace. A DMU from Edinburgh arrived at Hawick as *Pinza* rolled into the station, but there were few to witness this last day. Another photo-stop was made at Fountainhall, and Edinburgh Waverley was reached on time at 14.50.

Snow was falling as the special left for the south,

but it cleared as the train climbed into the hills. As we headed once more to the summit at Whitrope, and passed the desolate Riccarton Junction, it was hard to believe that on the following day the hills would never again reverberate to the sound of a hard-working locomotive.

The journey continued uninterrupted until Kershopefoot, where we came to a stand due to the level crossing gates being closed. We wondered if we had become involved in a local protest, but we eventually passed unhindered. The final train, the Edinburgh-St Pancras sleeper, had considerable trouble at Newcastleton, with the local population placing themselves across the line to block the train.

As can be seen from the log of the journey, the 'Deltic' gave some lively running back over the Settle and Carlisle line, but not as fast as on the outward trip. An on-time arrival at Leeds City was recorded at 20.48, thus ending the branch's first outing with a 'Deltic'.

SCHEDULE

M. Ch.						M. Ch.
—	dep. 09.30	Leeds City	...	...	20.48 arr.	211.15
0.75	09.33	Wortley Junction	...	...	20.45	210.20
10.56	09.43	Shipley (Leeds Junction)	...	...	20.36	200.39
16.79	09.53	Keighley	...	...	20.27	194.16
25.00	10.03	Snaygill	...	...	20.19	186.15
26.14	arr. 10.05	Skipton	...	...	20.16 dep.	
	dep. 10.07	Skipton	...	...	20.14 arr.	185.01
36.15	10.19	Hellifield	...	...	20.02	175.00
39.35	10.23½	Settle Junction	...	...	19.58½	171.60
53.35	10.46½	Blea Moor	...	...	19.45	157.60
64.50	10.57½	Ais Gill ...	...	...	19.35	146.45
82.15	11.13	Appleby	...	...	19.10	129.00
112.08	11.38½	Petteril Junction	...	...	18.37½	99.07
113.00	11L40½	Carlisle	...	...	18L35	
	11L42½	Carlisle	...	...	18L33	98.15
113.59	11.44½	Carlisle No. 3	...	...	18.29	97.36
114.27	11.47½	Canal Junction	...	...	18.26	96.68
122.46	11.58½	Longtown Junction	...	...	18.17	88.49
127.03	12.04	Riddings Junction	...	...	18.11	84.12
137.18	12.17	Newcastleton	...	...	17.59	73.77
145.27	arr. 12.34	Riccarton Junction	...	...	17.49	65.68
	dep. 12.44	Riccarton Junction	...	...		
158.28	arr. 13.07	Hawick	...	...	17.22	52.67
	dep. 13.17	Hawick	...	...		
170.50	13.32	St. Boswells	...	...	17.07	40.45
177.52	13.44	Galashiels	...	...	16.55	33.43
188.50	arr. 14.05	Fountainhall	...	...		
	dep. 14.15	Fountainhall	...	...		
192.06	14.23	Heriot	...	...	16.35	19.09
202.74	14.37	Hardengreen Junction	...	...	16.14	8.21
204.76	14.41	Millerhill	...	...	16.10	6.19
208.15	14.44	Portobello	...	...	16.06	3.00
211.15	arr. 14.50	Edinburgh Waverley	...	...	16.00 dep.	—

The tour paused again at Fountainhall for photographs. 'Deltic' No 7 *Pinza* was allocated to Finsbury Park for most of its working days, between June 1961 and December 1981, being cut up at Doncaster Works in August 1982. Latterly in its career it was to receive white surrounds to the cab roof, which was a feature of the Finsbury Park locomotives. *Gavin Morrison*

Just after arrival at Edinburgh Waverley, *Pinza* is seen prior to leaving for Haymarket depot, with the North British Hotel tower dominating the skyline. Inspector Geoff Wilson of Holbeck can be seen talking to passengers. *Gavin Morrison*

Appendix

Complete list of RCTS railtours in Great Britain and Ireland, 1938-69

Tours in **bold** are those included in this book. Motive power only listed for tours up to the end of 1967.

Date	Tour title	Motive power
11.9.38	Stirling Single	GNR 1
25.5.46	Longmoor	WD 75282
3.6.50	Corringham Light Railway	Avonside 0-6-0ST
2.7.50	RH&DR	*Typhoon*
30.9.50	Holborn Viaduct to Victoria	31102, 31722, 32418
14.5.51	East London No 1	E8619, 64647, 47300
16.6.51	Nottingham	67363
24.6.51	Bristol to South Wales	Railcar 20
12.7.51	Volks Electric Railway	Car 7
19.8.51	Bristol Rail Car	Railcar 16, 7015, 5325, 6369
29.3.52	North East London	1st train: 68549, 68613, 68644, 67731, 68783; 2nd train: 31507, 68575, 68549, 67739, 68787; Snow Hill banker 69435
11.5.52	South Yorks No 1	40487, 61166
18.5.52	Isle of Wight	W3, W32, W14
14.6.52	Bishops Waltham Branch	30589
22.6.52	Wye Valley & B&M Line	Railcar 24
5.10.52	Brighton Works Centenary Special	32424, 32636
19.10.52	Brighton Works Centenary Special	32425, 32636
11.10.52	Catterick Camp	69842
23.11.52	Bisley Tramway and North West Surrey	30577, 30027
17.5.53	Southampton Docks & Fawley Branch	30757, 30062
7.6.53	South Yorks No 2	62667, 64374, 26013
28.6.53	25th Anniversary Special	30464, 30711, 30583, 32662, 4056
26.7.53	Manchester and District	50644, 50855
6.9.53	East Anglian	62567, 64685, 62790
4.10.53	East Sussex	32390
10.10.53	Marylebone to Broad Street	69441, 69481, 40037, 45277
17.10.53	Warrington & District	67436
25.4.54	Swindon & Highworth	9011, 9023, 1366, 4707, 30517
25.4.54	Shropshire & M'shire Rly and Fairbourne Rly	WD167, FMR *Dingo*
16.5.54	**Lincolnshire**	**40935, 64199**
13.6.54	West Wales Diesel Car	Railcar 11, 4941
20.6.54	South Yorks No 3	64419, 65078, 60847
12.9.54	Invicta Special	31505, 31166, 31737, 31671, 68630, 68639
10.10.54	Buckinghamshire	30729, 58887
17.10.54	Liverpool & West Lancs	42664
6.2.55	**Hampshireman**	**32421, 32570, 32576, 30301, 30732**
30.4.55	Hertfordshire	61576, 68878, 49431, 41909
8.5.55	East Midlander No 1	61554, 45094
26.6.55	South Wales Diesel Car	Railcar 23
24.7.55	**The Fensman**	**70037, 65562**
24.7.55	RH&DR	*Northern Chief*
31.7.55	North Wales Light Railways	L&CEBR 19
13.8.55	Liverpool Overhead Rly	
14.8.55	The Wealden Limited	31019, 31048, 31177, 31737, 31764, 32426, 32416
24.9.55	Kegworth	84006

Date	Tour title	Motive power
2.10.55	North Wales	42461
11.3.56	Southend Centenary	LTSR 80
24.3.56	East London No 2	80080, 47484, 47351
6.5.56	East Midlander No 2	40454, 40489
8.7.56	Wessex Wyvern	30925, 30287, 1368, 4624, 6372, 32329
9.9.56	**Fensman No 2**	**61942, 42784, 65562, 61391, 11102, 61743**
15.9.56	Pennine Diesel	Four-car DMU
29.9.56	South Lancs Coalfield	47440, 41289
13.10.56	West London	42596
10.11.56	Hammersmith and Chiswick	42118, 80065
28.4.57	**North Somerset**	**30454, GWR 3440, 41202/3, 5528**
12.5.57	East Midlander No 3	62571
2.6.57	The Mercian	45511, 45091, 43018
23.6.57	**Yorkshire Coast**	**62387, 62731, 68246, 69881**
18.8.57	The Moonraker	GWR 3440, 5802
5.10.57	London Freight Lines	30687, 42686
29.3.58	London River	31518, 68646
13.4.58	Sussex Coast	32424, 80154, 30796
27.4.58	**Hertfordshire No 2**	**69614, 41901, 69632**
8.6.58	The Roses	Four-car DMU
10.8.58	Northern & Eastern	64656, 65440, 80041, 75055, 43245
21.9.58	South Yorkshire No 4	62660, 61165, 61127, 61126, 64222, 64268
4.10.58	**The Sapper**	**30120, WD 400**
21.3.59	**London & North Kent**	**69614, 69504, 68987, 31507, D8401**
4.4.59	South Lancs Freight Lines	42289
2.5.59	**Brunel Centenarian**	**7001, 5069**
2.5.59	Plymouth District	6240, 30182
9.8.59	The Grafton	D6101, 43474, 45139, 45091, 3646, 44833
6.9.59	Talyllyn Scenic	Eight-car DMU, *Edward Thomas*
19.9.59	Notts & Derbyshire	41320
26.9.59	Bristol & South Gloucestershire	9769
3.10.59	**London River No 2**	**31193**
26.3.60	Cheshire District	46472
7.5.60	**J21**	**65033**
12-17.6.60	Joint Scottish Tour	NBR 256, GNSR 49, HR 103, CR 123, 40663, 57594, 54485, 57441, 64615, 46463/4
24.7.60	**Dukeries**	**43145, 44590, 64314**
14.8.60	**The Greyhound**	**31768, 30718, 3737**
4.9.60	**The Cumbrian**	**MR 1000, 45503, 46442, 46456, *River Irt, River Esk***
10.9.60	Gypsum Mines	41280
11.9.60	East Midlander No 4	MR 1000, 7317, 76006
1.10.60	Northern Heights	Six-car DMU
12.10.60	Great Eastern Suburban	68619, 69687
9.4.61	Berks & Wilts	Six-car DMU
29.4.61	Vale of Belvoir	Three-car DMU
4-10.6.61	Joint Irish Tour	CIE 109, 119, 123, 131, 184, 461, 464, 560, 588, 603, 654, 801, B129, B132, GNR 85, 132, 174, UTA 26, 55, 65, 74
17.6.61	North Derbyshire	Two-car DMU
9.7.61	**The Borders**	**NBR 256, 46247, 60074, 60143, 61242, 61290, 64624**
9.9.61	Denton-Harlaxton	Three-car DMU
10.9.61	**M&SWJR**	**5306**
23.9.61	Four Counties	64420, 43763, 42372, E3058
20.1.62	**The Stainmore Limited**	**76049, 77003**
31.3.62	**Great Eastern Commemorative Steam**	**70003, 11168, 65567**
12.5.62	Groby	58148, three-car DMU
13.5.62	**East Midlander No 5**	**30925, 40646, 90348**
19.5.62	The Seven Companies	41273, 80117
2-3.6.62	**Aberdeen Flyer**	**60004, 60022GNSR 49, 65345, 46200, 46201**

Date	Tour title	Motive power
14-23.6.62	Joint Scottish Tour	CR 123, GNSR 49, HR 103, NBR 256, 42143, 42196, 42277, 42699, 42879, 44978, 55260, 57375, 57581, 78026, 80092, 80110, 80129, 64569, 65323, 65345, 65905
22.7.62	**Festiniog**	**40116, 40078, 45565, 46145, 46200, 73044, DMU**
25.8.62	The Fernie	42350, 41225, 44278
8-9.9.62	Isle of Man	MER 32, SMR 6
22.9.62	Mid Lancs	49451, 42844, 78036
29.6.62	Derbyshire Branch Lines	Five-car DMU
6.10.62	East London No 3	D8236
7.10.62	**The Sussex Special**	**30925, 32418, 32636, 32353**
2.12.62	**South Western Suburban**	**30585, 30587, 30517**
16.12.62	South Western Suburban	30535, 30587, 30517
30.3.63	Silvertown Tramway	D4192
27.4.63	The Cheshire Rambler	61039, 44548
27.4.63	North Cornishman & Camel Valleyman	LSWR 120, 1369
4.5.63	**The Dalesman**	**LNER 3442**
11.5.63	The North Midlands	34006, 61004, 48519
18.5.63	The Joint Lines	45238, 42087, 44414
30.6.63	**The Three Summits**	**60004, 60023, 46255, 57581, HR 103**
21.7.63	Gloucestershire	6841, 82036, 6993, 1020, PBA *Bristol*
27.9-1.10.63	North Eastern	46409, 44467, 46238, 62024, 63460, 62027, 61037, 67620, 43057, 43129, 42405, 61018, 61031, 61435, D2046
5.10.63	The Duchess Commemorative	46251, 42414
13.10.63	East Midlander No 6	42896, 44774
19.10.63	**The Nidd Valley**	**42409**
9.11.63	Wansbeck Wanderer	43129
22.3.64	**The Sussex Downsman**	**33027, 31411, 34066, 41287**
25.4.64	**North Yorkshireman**	**61435, 44790, 67646, 42639, 60855**
2.5.64	North Eastern Limited	60051
3.5.64	**The Cornubian**	**2887, 34002**
9.5.64	**East Midlander No 7**	**46251, 34038, 30071**
23.5.64	**Ribble-Lune**	**72007, 46441**
30.5.64	North Staffs	45020
2-3.6.64	Joint Isle of Man	DCT 1, MER 5, IMR 8
3-13.6.64	Joint Steam Tour of Ireland	CIE 130, 183, 186, 198, E431, GNR 170, 207, UTA 7, 60, 97
13.6.64	**The Solway Ranger**	**35012, 45394, 46426, 46458, CR 123, GNSR 49, DMU**
20.6.64	Glasson Dock	46433
27.6.64	**High Peak No 1**	**61360, 26000, 68006, 68012, 68079, 47006**
29.8.64	High Peak No 2	61158, 26000, 68006, 68012, 68079, 47006
6.9.64	West Riding	Five-car DMU
12.9.64	Notts & Lincs	44918
19.9.64	Wenford	1369
26.9.64	**The Scottish Lowlander**	**46256, 60007, 60009**
10.10.64	Hull Docks	DMU
18.10.64	The Midhurst Belle	30839, 30064, 30530, 35007
24.10.64	Jubilee Requiem	60009
9.1.65	**Derwent Valley Light Railway**	**D2111**
16.1.65	Derwent Valley Light Railway	D2111
13.2.65	**Rebuilt Scot**	**46115, 44822**
21.3.65	**Tyne Solway**	**60131**
27.3.65	Exmoor Ranger	41206, 41291, 3205
10.4.65	North Eastern No 2	LNER 3442, 92097, 62027, eight-car DMU
22.5.65	Cheshire Lines Centenary	44735, 42587
29.5.65	**East Midlander No 8**	**LNER 4472**
28.8.65	Fife Coast	NBR 256, 64569
19.9.65	**Blyth & Tyne**	**60004, 43057, D6769**
25-26.9.65	West Wales	3654, 9609, 1643, 1669, 6859
2.10.65	North Lincs	70012
16.10.65	Midland Locos Requiem	43953, D8613

Date	Tour title	Motive power
23.10.65	**South Yorkshire No 5**	**48202, D5561**
4.12.65	Jubilee Commemorative	45654, 45596
2.1.66	**Somerset & Dorset**	**35011, 34015, 31639, 48309, 31283, 41307**
6.3.66	Somerset & Dorset Farewell	35028, 41283, 41249, 34013, 34057, D7014
20.3.66	**The Solent**	**34089, 75070, 30064, 30073, 31639**
26.3.66	The Eight Counties	48467, 61302, 26000, 45596, D5016, E3093
16.4.66	**Longmoor**	**31639, 31411, 77014, AD 600, AD 195, AD 196**
23.4.66	St George	46519, 78036, 42727
30.4.66	Longmoor	31639, 31791, 73114, AD 600, AD 195, AD 196, AD 878
14.5.66	Central Wales Scenic	Six-car DMU
21.5.66	East Midlander No 9	92077, 43026
13.8.66	Great Central	34002, 48197, 61131, 26053
24.9.66	South Lancs	45154
1.10.66	Notts & Yorks	44825, D5568
29.10.66	Stoke Area Brake Van	41204
5.3.67	North Eastern Region MPDs	Four-car DMU
19.3.67	**The Lancastrian**	**70015**
29.4.67	WM&CQR	92058, 42616, 42647, 48697
6.5.67	**North Eastern No 3**	**45562, D6778**
18.6.67	**Farewell to Southern Steam**	**73029, 34023, 34089, 34108, 80146, 35013**
16.7.67	**A4 to Glasgow**	**60019**
29.7.67	Ten Counties Scenic	Three-car DMU
7.10.67	Grimsby/Inningham	Two-car DMU
21.10.67	East London No 4	Six-car DMU
28.10.67	The Border Limited	LNER 4498, 44767, 45295, 44690, 45196, D145
4.11.67	A4 to Edinburgh	60019
4.11.67	Edinburgh Local	Four-car DMU
25.11.67	The Three Spires	Three-car DMU
9.3.68	West London Junctions	
16.3.68	Cumbrian Rover	
6.4.68	Thames and Avon	
20.4.68	Lancastrian No 2	
18.5.68	South Midlands	
16.6.68	**Dalesman No 2**	
4.8.68	End of Steam Commemorative	
14.9.68	Bicester and Thames Valley	
5.10.68	Doncaster Decoy	
12.10.68	East Manchester	
26.10.68	Moorlands	
23.11.68	Black Countryman	
5.1.69	**Farewell to the Waverley Route**	
1.3.69	London Suburban	
19.4.69	Forester	
3.5.69	Cambrian Scenic	
4.5.69	Tyseley Steam Rally Special	
31.5.69	Cheddar Valley Scenic	
23.8.69	Bulmers and Welsh Border	
27.9.69	Keighley and Worth and Middleton	
4.10.69	Lincolnshire Coast	
11.10.69	Festiniog	
22.11.69	The Reunion	

Index of locations